THE PHILOSOPHY OF
LOCKE
AND
HOBBES

SUGWON KANG
DEPARTMENT OF POLITICAL SCIENCE
CITY UNIVERSITY OF NEW YORK

Simon & Schuster, Inc.
15 Columbus Circle
New York, NY 10023

Monarch and colophons are trademarks
of Simon & Schuster, registered in the
U.S. Patent and Trademark Office.

ISBN: 0-671-00531-6

Library of Congress Catalog Card Number: 66-27745

Printed in the United States of America

CONTENTS

PREFACE

This commentary covers Books I and II of Hobbes' *Leviathan* and Locke's *Treatise of Civil Government,* which contain the authors' chief political ideas. It is fitting that Hobbes and Locke should be considered together for at least three reasons. First, they are probably the two greatest political philosophers England ever produced. Second, they lived only a generation or two apart. Their lives put end to end span the turbulent seventeenth century (Hobbes was born in 1588; Locke died in 1704), a century that saw the fall of monarchy, its restoration, and its final adjustment with the demands for freedom of the rising middle class. Third, and perhaps most important, there are several points on which they see eye to eye. Locke was a promising student in London when Hobbes' greatest work, the *Leviathan,* first appeared in print. Locke read it carefully, and it surely had an enormous influence on his own thinking. Many of its views he adopted as his own—the essential rationality of man, the theories of natural right, natural law, the state of nature, and the social contract. Both Hobbes and Locke believed that the state existed as an artificial creation of man to protect and preserve the interests of the individual. This stress on individualism constituted a radical departure from the tradition of political philosophy, which looked upon the state either as the highest ethical good, an object of love and patriotism, or as a divinely ordained instrument of restraint and discipline, which men were to submit to with awe and religious reverence.

Summaries such as those that follow—no matter how good—are at best only a guide to and not a substitute for the original works. The reader is therefore advised to make this the starting point of his investigation of the ideas of these two great philosophers, and to read for himself how these ideas are expressed. An effort has been made to present appropriate quotations from the texts to give the reader a flavor of the authors' writing styles.

Finally, the reader should be warned that no philosopher is immune from criticism. They all contradict themselves at one time or other in the course of their writings. We should only ask how does the contradiction come about? and how serious is it? To the extent possible, these contradictions have been exposed, not in the spirit of showing up the philosopher, but in the interest of academic integrity. It is hoped this will serve not to confuse the reader, but to strengthen his critical faculties.

THOMAS HOBBES: INTRODUCTORY

LIFE AND TIMES

EARLY LIFE: Hobbes was born two months premature near Malmesbury, England, on April 5, 1588, a day on which the Spanish Armada was nearing the English coast. His mother's fright at the approaching fleet is said to have been responsible for the early birth. Late in life, Hobbes said of the occasion that his mother "brought forth twins—myself and fear."

It has been suggested that fear was Hobbes' lifelong companion. There's a famous passage in the *Leviathan* where he speaks of the obligation of subjects to bear arms for the sovereign, but he is willing to make exception "for natural timorousness, not only to women . . . but to men of feminine courage." Scholars tend to suspect that Hobbes counted himself among the men of feminine courage, and therefore an unsuitable candidate for military duty. In a more serious vein, it should be pointed out that fear is the key passion in Hobbes' political system, which uses the human passions as its foundation.

Hobbes' father was a poor, boorish, and ignorant vicar, who one day lost his job for quarreling with a neighboring pastor at the church door. He fled in disgrace, leaving his wife and three children behind him. The vicar's brother, a prosperous glover, looked after the children. He became especially interested in the precocious young Thomas, who at the age of four was able to read and write, at six learned Greek and Latin, and at fourteen translated Euripides' *Medea* into Latin iambics.

When he was fifteen, Hobbes entered Oxford, which was described by a contemporary as a place where young men became debauched. The youthful Hobbes turned out to be something of a problem student. He had no use for the university, or for the Aristotelian and Scholastic philosophy taught there. Throughout his life, Hobbes, who must have inherited some of his father's irascible temper, heaped scorn upon the English universities with

their "vapid" curricula, and attacked Aristotle as the purveyor
of "erroneous doctrines." But he owed more to both than he
would ever acknowledge.

INFLUENCES: In 1610, now twenty-two and in spite of himself the holder of an Oxford degree, Hobbes started an association with the aristocratic Cavendish family that was to have an
enormous impact upon his life. The Cavendishes (the Earls of
Devonshire) were extremely influential. Through them, he met
Bacon, Harvey, and other great men of his time. It was with
Lord Hardwick, later the second Earl of Devonshire—whom he
was hired to tutor and soon befriended—that he first embarked
on a tour of Europe. He returned there many times during the
course of his life. On the Continent, Hobbes was exposed to the
works of Galileo and Kepler. He later visited Galileo in Florence.
While in Paris, where he lived many years, his circle of ac-
quaintances included the mathematician Mersenne and the
philosopher Descartes. Hobbes was among those privileged to
read Descartes' *Meditations* before publication. He wrote objections to it, which Descartes published with rebuttals as an
appendix. Descartes thought little of Hobbes as a metaphysician,
but upon reading *De Cive* declared him to be the foremost political philosopher of the day.

WORKS: When Hobbes returned to England in 1637, he
had decided to develop a systematic theory of politics. Up to
that time his published works consisted of a translation of
Thucydides and some abstracts of Aristotle. He was nearly fifty,
but his greatest achievements still lay ahead.

So he set to work and produced a preliminary sketch of his
political system. This was passed around to his immediate circle
of friends, but not published at the time. The ideas it contained
were radical, and this was no time for radical ideas. England
was in turmoil. The parliament was becoming increasingly bolder
in its challenge to royal power. Tensions would soon erupt into
bloody civil war, which was destined to end in the victory of
Cromwell's Parliamentary forces and the downfall of the mon-

archy. Hobbes, whose own leanings were monarchist, feared that his political views would get him into trouble, and in 1640 hurried back to Paris where he sat out the war.

There he wrote *De Cive*, which he published in 1642. *De Cive* is the first full exposition of Hobbes' views on government and the obligations of citizens. It promptly infuriated the clergy for what they considered to be its atheism in putting secular above ecclesiastical authority. So passionate was their attack that it cost Hobbes his job tutoring the future King Charles II, then exiled in Paris.

So Hobbes set to work on *Leviathan*, which includes not only two dispassionate sections on man and society, but also a highly emotional and virulent attack against the forces of religion, which he refers to irreverently as "The Kingdom of Darkness." Needless to say, *Leviathan* met with disapproval. It angered royalists in exile, who thought it a justification of Cromwell and it angered the clergy, both English and French, for its prejudice against the church.

Once again, Hobbes was forced to flee from danger. This time he made his way secretly across the Channel to London, where he declared his submission to Cromwell and withdrew from politics. The restoration of the Stuarts in 1660 also brought the restoration of Hobbes' favor with his sovereign. Charles II, who had been his personal friend, even granted Hobbes a monthly pension, but never got around to paying it, possibly because of the clergy's continuing animosity toward the philosopher.

OLD AGE: Hobbes remained active in his old age. He had always fancied himself a mathematician, and he occupied himself a great deal of the time in a futile effort to square the circle. Once he became locked in a controversy with an Oxford mathematician named John Wallis, and got much the worse of it. He also spent some time carping at the universities for teaching the "false" principles of the classic philosophers, rather than his own. When he was eighty-four he wrote his autobiography in

Latin verse, and in the next two years translated the *Iliad* and *Odyssey* of Homer.

Hobbes was a good-sized man, over six feet tall, red-haired, hot-tempered, generous, witty, and a congenial social companion. He is said to have walked every day and sung every night. At seventy-five, he still played an occasional game of tennis. He admitted to being drunk a hundred times during his life, and, although never married, had one illegitimate daughter, for whom he provided conscientiously.

He died on December 4, 1679, in Hardwick at the age of ninety-one, after a trip from Chatsworth had sapped his strength and brought on an attack of paralysis.

PHILOSOPHY

MATERIALISM: Hobbes' philosophy has been commonly described as "materialistic." He was greatly influenced by Galileo's mechanistic approach to science. Hobbes conceived of the universe as a gigantic machine governed by the laws of motion. Matter and motion are thought to be the lowest common denominators of reality. Consequently, bodies and their movements are the only legitimate subject matter of philosophy.

Thus, Hobbes' own philosophy has three major divisions: *physics,* the study of moving bodies; *psychology,* the study of the human nervous system; and *politics,* the study of many human nervous systems interacting. These divisions are represented in the titles of three major works: *De Corpore* (On Bodies), *De Homine* (On Man), and *De Cive* (On the State). The first two parts of *Leviathan,* the most important of all Hobbes' works, are devoted to the study of man and the state, respectively.

METHOD: It is generally recognized that Hobbes was greatly influenced by Euclidean geometry. Although geometry is that branch of mathematics which deals specifically with the relations of points, lines, planes, and solids in space, Hobbes seems to use the term "geometry" in a broad sense to include the entire gamut of mathematical sciences. In any case, it is certain that Hobbes thought geometry to be something glamorous. In Chapter IV of the *Leviathan,* for instance, he tells us that geometry is "the only science that it hath pleased God hitherto to bestow on Mankind." And in the following chapter he argues that geometry is the only science that has attained indisputable conclusions: "For there is not one of them that begins his ratiocination from the definitions, or explications of the names they are to use; which is a method that hath been used only in geometry; whose conclusions have been made indisputable."

Hobbes' intellectual ambition was to explain all phenomena, including those of man and his government, in terms of matter and motion, and with mathematical precision. But, as an eminent scholar has shown, much of Hobbes' political thought had been formed in his youth, prior to his intellectual conversion to the science of geometry. Be that as it may, the fact that Hobbes tried to follow the mathematical method in his own examination of politics is beyond question. He started from a set of first principles (or "propositions," as they are called in geometry), i.e., matter and motion, and then tried to explain all other phenomena from their interaction.

PSYCHOLOGY AND POLITICS: Hobbes' conception of politics (man in society) is based on his conception of psychology (individual man). According to his materialist psychology, human conduct is a product of human passions, and passions result from a response to motions from external objects. Hobbes says the most dominant passions are fear of violent death and desire for power. These, however, are mere manifestations of man's most basic impulse, which Hobbes calls the urge of *self-preservation*. Hobbes asserts that this basic impulse is a right of the individual. He calls it a *natural right.*

According to Hobbes, this instinct of self-preservation, or so-called natural right, is possessed by all men equally. So broad is its application that it gives men the right to do all things necessary to that preservation, including the right to subdue or destroy others, or possess their goods. But it is obvious that if everyone possesses the right to all things, it comes to nothing, because such total liberty for everyone can only lead to mutual destruction. This is what Hobbes actually conceives the natural state, or condition, of man to be—a state of war of every man against every man, in which their lives are "solitary, poor, nasty, brutish and short."

But the instinct for self-preservation gives men also the inclination for peace. Thus, the passion of fear—fear of violent death—is still operating. It leads men in the state of war to desire peace. This is where reason comes into play. Reason *suggests* "articles of peace," once man's instinct for self-preservation indicates that peace is the goal to be achieved. So it turns out that man's peace-inclining passions overcome his war-inclining passions, and reason supplements the dominant passions. It is a victory, not for any one individual, but for the many individuals taken together.

The culmination of the reasoning process, so far as Hobbes' system is concerned, is the *social contract.* According to Hobbes, the social contract is the foundation of commonwealth, and, indeed, of all civilization. It comes about when reason directs each man to relinquish his natural right to all things on condition that every other man do the same. Then, since a contract is not a contract unless it can be enforced, reason directs that all parties to the contract agree to set up a sovereign power, with absolute and unconditional authority, to ensure that all parties live up to their part of the contract. The sovereign may be one man or an assembly—Hobbes prefers one man; but it is essential that the sovereign power be unrestricted. The sovereign is the executive, legislative, and judicial power all in one. As legislator and the sole source of law the sovereign determines what is just and unjust, right and wrong, as dictated by the needs of a harmonious social life.

Those who do not voluntarily enter into the social contract, and remain outside of commonwealth, are not bound by the commands of the sovereign, and continue to be in a state of war with one another. This, in fact, according to Hobbes, is the condition in which independent nations find themselves in their relations to one another—in a state of war without benefit of a sovereign power to settle their differences and assure their peace and security.

PLACE IN HISTORY

Like most great thinkers, Hobbes never seems to have doubted his greatness. In fact, he believed himself to be the first true political philosopher, the first to produce a theory of government on a scientific basis. All other philosophers in the entire tradition of political philosophy, he thought, had failed to do so.

Hobbes' reputation as a philosopher rests on his contribution to psychology, the theory of knowledge, and especially politics. In the first two categories, his influence was immediate. His theory of human passion and appetite can be traced in the philosophy of Spinoza. His psychology also guided Joseph Butler and Francis Hutcheson, among other English thinkers, in their search for the proper understanding of human motivation. And his theory of knowledge must surely have exerted a tremendous influence not only on Locke but also on Hume.

As a political thinker, however, Hobbes suffered a long period of ill-repute, especially during the time immediately following Locke. Hobbes' unpopularity, which stemmed from his leanings toward absolute monarchy, continued through the eighteenth century of Hume, Rousseau, and Burke. Early in the nineteenth century, however, an interest in his thought was revived by the so-called Philosophical Radicals. Bentham seems to have been greatly impressed with both Hobbes' psychological and economic views, while James Mill found in Hobbes an inspiration for his principles of associationist psychology. Perhaps most important of all, John Austin made use of Hobbes' theory of sovereignty and law as the foundation for his analytical jurisprudence.

Since Austin's time, Hobbes has been gradually acknowledged in many circles as the founder of modern political theory—although some would reserve that honor for Machiavelli. In any case, Hobbes' place in English tradition is very high. One scholar spoke for most when he said, "Hobbes was probably the greatest writer on political philosophy that the English-speaking peoples have produced."

LEVIATHAN: PARTS I AND II

THE INTRODUCTION

Hobbes proclaims his thoroughgoing materialism at the beginning of *Leviathan*. Life is "but a motion of limbs," and if this be so, he asks, "why may we not say that all *automata* (engines that move themselves by springs and wheels as doth a watch) have an artificial life?" Moreover, "what is the heart, but a spring; and the nerves, but so many strings; and the joints but so many wheels, giving motion to the whole body. . . ?"

The commonwealth or state, which Hobbes calls "Leviathan" after the mythological sea monster of the Old Testament (Job 41), is a creation of art. In fact, Hobbes says, it is an "artificial man." This artificial man contains an artificial soul, the sovereignty, which gives life and motion to the whole body. It was God who created man, says Hobbes, but it is man who by means of pacts and covenants, created the body politic.

> **COMMENT:** In the first part of *Leviathan,* entitled "Of Man" Hobbes deals with the nature of man, his processes of learning and his passions. But his concepts are developed, so to speak, from the ground up, piece by piece, with painstaking care, until a great structure, or system, emerges; each part seemingly an integral and necessary element of the whole. But the student must see for himself, and one can only hope that this outline will serve to give the barest impression of Hobbes' achievement.

PART I. OF MAN

CHAPTER I. OF SENSE

First, we (Hobbes and his readers) focus on man singly in his physical environment. Here is man and there are objects outside of man. How does *he* perceive *them?* The answer is that he perceives them through his senses. But that leads to another question: What is the cause of sense perception?

This, in turn, leads to an exposition of Hobbes' most fundamental principle, namely, that all things are either matter or motion. The external object is matter, and it sends off waves of motion. To envision this more clearly, conceive of a pebble thrown into a pond. As it strikes the surface it sends off waves in all directions. Hobbes believed that waves come off all objects in all directions, and, if we are within range, the waves will press against our sensory organs of sight, hearing, feeling, smelling, and tasting, and thence to the brain and heart. The brain and heart, being also matter, produce motions outward, which raise an image of the external object. Thus, Hobbes defines sense as a "seeming to be some matter without." To put the definition in more modern terms, sense is perception of some outside matter, or object.

> **COMMENT:**   Hobbes makes it clear that his own conception of the sense-object relationship is at variance with the classical conception. Aristotle believed that an aspect of the object perceived actually entered into us—an aspect he called the object's "visible species" or "audible species," etc., depending on the sense involved. Moreover, according to Aristotle, the cause of understanding is that the thing understood gives off an "intelligible species."

CHAPTER II.   OF IMAGINATION

Hobbes tells us that a body once in motion moves forever. This explains, says Hobbes, why the sense impression remains with us even after the external object is removed from our immediate presence.

But over a period of time the sense impression fades. Hobbes says it decays—not as wood rotting away, but in becoming more obscure because of the interference of other sense impressions. Thus, after the stimulus of sense has taken place, there remain in the mind gradually fading relics of sensation. Decaying sense

Hobbes identifies as *imagination,* which is the same as *memory,* except that we would use the latter expression to signify the fact of fading or decaying. The memory of many things is *experience.* The imagination raised by words or other voluntary signs is *understanding.*

CHAPTER III. OF THE CONSEQUENCE OR TRAIN OF IMAGINATIONS

Hobbes has established by now that sense is the basis of thought. We do not have thoughts without first receiving an impression through our senses—either in the immediate or distant past. But we receive many sense impressions, not just one. During our waking hours, they come constantly, one right after another. So it is that a sequence of imaginations is raised within us. This sequence is called *train of thought,* or *mental discourse.*

Hobbes distinguishes two kinds of mental discourse: (1) unguided, which is of no importance, and (2) regulated. *Regulated mental discourse* has some end, or goal, in sight. We conceive of the means to achieve the end, and turn the means into action on our part toward the goal.

We may do two things in regulated mental discourse: (1) seek *causes* of things imagined, or (2) seek to know the *consequences* of what we imagine. By these methods (kinds of regulated discourse) we conceive of means to achieve a desired end.

Another important concept in the realm of mind is *prudence.* Prudence is a presumption either of things to come or of things past based on experience. For example, if we stand out in the rain many times and each time get wet, we might preseume that if we stand out in the rain at some time in the future we will once again get wet. This kind of presumption Hobbes calls "foresight." If, on the other hand, we learn from past experience that each time it rains the ground becomes wet, and we arise one morning to find the ground wet, we might presume that it rained during the night. Our presumption in the first case is of something in the future; in the second, of something in the past.

COMMENT: The student must not construe prudence to mean science. Prudence, for Hobbes, is not science, but natural wisdom. Like the other activities of the mind discussed so far, prudence only suggests man's receptive powers. Its cause is sheer sensation, and it is but a form of movement in the brain.

CHAPTER IV.   OF SPEECH

"The most noble and profitable invention" of mankind, says Hobbes, is *speech*. It is through speech that we distinguish man from beasts. Speech is used to transfer a train of thought into words. Through speech we produce *names,* and through names we discover all that is universal. Furthermore, without speech, or language, there would be no truth or falsehood, for "true" and "false" are attributes of speech. Without language we would have no science, for it is language that allows us to make definitions, which are the starting points of all science.

COMMENT: Hobbes considers geometry to be the one genuine science so far created, because only in geometry do we find the proper use of definitions.

The theory that universals are not real, but are only names or words, and that reality is limited to particulars is known in philosophy as "nominalism." Hobbes' philosophy is an excellent example of nominalism. For Hobbes there is nothing universal but names, and without words we could not conceive of general ideas.

CHAPTER V.   OF REASON AND SCIENCE

We come now to the ultimate movement of the mind, *reason,* which is made possible through speech. We may define reason as the evaluating ("reckoning") of consequences of general names which are widely known through speech. To reason, we proceed from one consequence to the next. The consequences are then reduced to general rules, which we call theorems.

Hobbes draws a parallel of reasoning in words, as just described, with reasoning in numbers, as in mathematics. Here the influence of Euclidean geometry on Hobbes' thought is evident.

It is important to note that reason, according to Hobbes, is not innate. That is, we are not born reasonable creatures. Nor is reason attained by experience, as is prudence. Rather, reason is attained by industry, i.e., hard work; and this in two ways: (1) by making apt definitions, and (2) by following orderly method. The orderly method consists in "proceeding from the elements [names to assertions made by connecting one name to another], and so to syllogisms ['connexions of assertions'], till we come to a knowledge of all the consequences of names appertaining to the subject in hand." It is this knowledge, says Hobbes, which is called "science."

CHAPTER VI. OF THE INTERIOR BEGINNINGS OF VOLUNTARY MOTIONS; COMMONLY CALLED THE PASSIONS; AND THE SPEECHES BY WHICH THEY ARE EXPRESSED

COMMENT: In addition to the intellectual, or mental processes of man, which we have been discussing, Hobbes also speaks of another set of movements in the brain, which he calls comprehensively the "active" powers of man. These are the emotions, or passions. Hobbes' account of the passions is lengthy and taxonomical, and we can only summarize his main arguments.

Hobbes refers to the passions as "voluntary" movements. They are distinguished fundamentally from such things as blood circulation, pulse, breathing, etc., which Hobbes calls "involuntary" or "vital" movements. The difference is this: involuntary movements move without interruption and are not affected by imagination; voluntary movements are constantly subject to interruption and move in direct response to ideas, or images. In other words, voluntary movements have their beginnings in imagination.

So it is, says Hobbes, that "because *going, speaking,* and the like voluntary motions depend always upon a precedent thought of *whither, which way,* and *what,* it is evident that the imagination is the first internal beginning of all voluntary motion."

Now we may explore the voluntary motions in greater depth. The undifferentiated form of the voluntary motions Hobbes calls *endeavor.* These forms are the "small beginnings of motion within the body . . . before they appear in walking, speaking . . . and other visible actions. . . ." Endeavor toward something which causes it is *appetite,* or *desire.* Endeavor away from an object is called *aversion. Love* corresponds to desire, and *hate* to aversion. Accordingly, whatever is the object of a man's desire, he will call *good,* and whatever he dislikes he will call *evil.*

> **COMMENT:**   The doctrine of ethical subjectivism could not be expressed in clearer terms. Hobbes is saying that nothing is good or evil, right or wrong, in itself—that one's personal feelings are the ultimate criteria of what is good and right. Different men desire different things, each calling the object of his desire "good" and the object of his aversion "evil." In fact, Hobbes tells us, the same man will at different times love and hate the same thing.

Pleasure and *displeasure* are also different kinds of movement in the brain. Pleasure accompanies the sensation of an object considered good; displeasure accompanies the image of an "evil" object. Hobbes tells us now that the person considering the object is alternately attracted to or repulsed from it. That is, he has alternating appetite and aversion. He is constantly weighing good and evil, pleasant and unpleasant, consequences. This succession of alternating emotions in the mind is called *deliberation.* Ultimately, one must make a choice. He must either accept or reject the thing about which he deliberates. The end of deliberation, "the last appetite in deliberating," Hobbes calls *will.* In other words, when a decision is reached, after a process of deliberation (which signifies the stage of indecision), a man's desire is fixed upon a definite object, and then he is said to "will" that object.

> **COMMENT:** Note the remarkable parallel—which, I am certain, is intentional—between the notion that "will" is the end of the succession of emotions (deliberation) and his previous observation that "prudence" is the end of the succession of images in the brain (mental discourse).
>
> Hobbes' definition of will is in sharp contrast to that of Aristotle. According to Aristotle, whose view was to be accepted by the Scholastics, will necessarily involves *rational* choice, i.e., an act of *reason*. Consequently, for Aristotle, irrational persons like the feebleminded, the intoxicated, and so on, are incapable of willing.
>
> Hobbes, of course, says they can, and that it is absurd to say they cannot. He points out that we often do things either against or without reason. This applies even to adults without serious mental defects. Thus Hobbes rids the will of its rational element.
>
> The idea that will is nothing but the last appetite in deliberation suggests that man does not rise above his passions, and, in fact, is bound by his passions in making his choice. Whether one accepts as good or rejects as bad any particular object is determined by which passion is strongest within him. In this context, Hobbes is said to reject the notion of "free will."

Furthermore, Hobbes tells us there is no such thing in life as "perpetual tranquillity of mind," because life itself, he says, "is but motion, and can never be without desire, nor without fear, no more than without sense." Consequently, what man seeks is not any settled object, but rather "continual success in obtaining those things which a man from time to time desires, that is to say, continual prospering." This process of success is called *felicity,* and involves motion rather than rest.

COMMENT: Here again we find Hobbes' revolutionary break with classical and medieval philosophy—in this instance, with the Aristotelian notion of the *summum bonum*. We will have more to say about Hobbes' dynamic concept of happiness in Chapter XI.

CHAPTER VII.   OF THE ENDS, OR RESOLUTIONS OF DISCOURSE

Deliberation and discourse are similar except that deliberation accompanies the passions, while discourse is part of our mental processes. With deliberation there is alternating attraction to or revulsion from an object, and a final act of will. With discourse there is alternating presumption of truth or falsehood (called *opinion*), and a final opinion in search of truth (called *judgment*). Judgment, the end of discourse, cannot be absolute. It is conditional—although, ultimately, it is based on facts which are absolute. The facts are perceived through the senses. Judgment is gained through discourse. It is only through discourse that we can rise to science. But we must first put our impressions into words, so that we may draw conclusions. A *conclusion* is a judgment put into words. When we have drawn conclusions, we will have *science,* which is "conditional knowledge" of consequences of words.

COMMENT: Until recently, the terms "philosophy" and "science" have been used interchangeably. Nowadays when we say "philosophy" we normally mean such disciplines as logic, ethics, metaphysics, theory of knowledge, and aesthetics. "Science" generally refers to the natural sciences (e.g., biology and physics), or the social sciences (e.g., political science or sociology).

Philosophy in the broader traditional sense had to do with investigation and classification of general facts or principles of reality. These facts and principles might concern anything from nature to man to society. At the time of

Socrates there existed no clear division of knowledge. Philosophy had to do with all kinds of learning, and was distinguished only from the practical arts, such as the art of persuasion or the art of governing. Aristotle attempted to classify the various fields of knowledge, but in spite of his efforts the term "philosophy" retained its general meaning down through medieval times. Only law, medicine, and theology were excluded from its wide embrace.

It was not till the eighteenth and early nineteenth centuries that the division of philosophy became generally accepted. The two major fields were (1) natural philosophy (now called physical or natural science) and (2) moral philosophy (which today includes philosophy in its limited sense, plus psychology and the social sciences). Even then, the terms "philosophy" and "science" got mixed up. Harvey and Newton, for example, were called "natural philosophers," while Hume and Adam Smith were later known as "moral scientists."

To go back to Hobbes' definition of science as "conditional knowledge," he obviously does not refer to the natural and social sciences we know today. Rather, he meant science in the traditional sense as philosophy in general. What he means to say is that philosophy has to do with hypothetical generalizations and conclusions about the names of things, and does not delve into the nature of things. Or, as the eminent Hobbesian commentator Michael Oakeshott has put it, philosophy, for Hobbes, is but an "establishment by reasoning of true fictions." It is in this sense that it must remain "conditional knowledge."

CHAPTER VIII. OF THE VIRTUES COMMONLY CALLED INTELLECTUAL; AND THEIR CONTRARY DEFECTS

In this chapter Hobbes discusses the origins and nature of *wit*. He says there are two kinds of wit: *natural* and *acquired*. To speak of "natural wit" is not, however, to say that wit is born with us. Rather, it comes to us by experience and use only— that is to say, without culture and training. It consists of "swift imagining and steady direction to some approved end."

By "acquired wit" Hobbes means that wit which is cultivated through training. It is grounded on the right use of speech. Reason alone belongs in this category. As we have already noted, reason is based on the right use of speech and produces science.

We have all observed the different degrees of wit in people. What accounts for it? Hobbes' answer is that differences of wit in people are caused by differences in their passions—which in turn are due partly to bodily differences and partly to educational differences. Most important of the passions affecting wit are the desires for *power, riches, knowledge,* and *honor.* These, says Hobbes, can be reduced to just one—the desire for power, because riches, knowledge, and honor are but different kinds of *power.*

CHAPTER IX.   OF THE SEVERAL SUBJECTS OF KNOWLEDGE

Hobbes adduces two kinds of knowledge: (1) knowledge of fact, and (2) "knowledge of the consequence of one affirmation to another." The first is mere sensation and memory, and is absolute because it is the mere register of facts in the mind. The second is science, and is conditional, as was explained in the comment to Chapter VII.

The register of knowledge of fact is called history, of which there are two kinds: (1) natural history and (2) civil history. The registers of science are the books which contain "the demonstrations of consequences of one affirmation to another"— commonly called "books of philosophy."

This chapter also includes a comprehensive diagram of the various subdivisions of science, or philosophy.

CHAPTER X. OF POWER, WORTH, DIGNITY, HONOR, AND WORTHINESS

Power is defined as a present means of obtaining some future apparent good. It is of two kinds: (1) *natural,* or original, and (2) *instrumental.* Natural power is eminence of bodily or mental faculties—e.g., "extraordinary strength, form, prudence, arts, eloquence, liberality, nobility." Instrumental power is the means to more power, and Hobbes lists as examples riches, reputation, friends, or good luck. The greatest of human powers is several powers compounded and united by consent, in one person "that has the use of all their powers depending on his will—such as is the power of a commonwealth."

The *worth* of a man is defined as his price—that is, "so much as would be given for the use of his power." *Honor* is the manifestation of a man's value. *Dignity* is a man's public worth (his public office or title) as set by the commonwealth. Hobbes continues his discussion of power in the following chapter.

CHAPTER XI. OF THE DIFFERENCE OF MANNERS

There are three points of importance in this chapter. First, according to Hobbes, there is no *summum bonum,* or supreme good, in life. (The *summum bonum* in classical philosophy is usually conceived as that in which all other goods are included, or from which they are derived.) *Felicity,* or happiness, says Hobbes, is a "continual progress of the desire, from one object to another; the attaining of the former being still but the way to the latter." The reason for this, we are told, is that "the object of man's desire is not to enjoy once only . . . but to assure forever the way of his future desire."

> **COMMENT:** We see again a break with classical and medieval philosophy. Both Aristotle and St. Thomas Aquinas adhered to a conception of static and perfect happiness. Aristotle, for instance, in the *Nicomachean Ethics* (X,7), speaks of the activity of contemplation, or intel-

lectual life, as forming "pure" or "perfect" happiness. However, for Hobbes, this is not possible. He says happiness involves continual progress; it consists in prospering, not in having prospered. In such a dynamic and relativistic conception of happiness, there can be no *summum bonum,* or final tranquillity of mind.

Second, Hobbes puts as a universal inclination of men "a perpetual and restless desire of power after power, that ceaseth only in death." This means not so much that we have an unbounded lust for power as that we try to acquire more, to safeguard the power we already have, without which we cannot live well.

COMMENT: We can readily see the implications of this doctrine, especially when applied to international politics. One is reminded of an insightful statement by the contemporary theologian Reinhold Niebuhr in his important book, *Moral Man and Immoral Society.* Niebuhr says, "Every group, as every individual, has expansive desires which are rooted in the instinct of survival and soon extend beyond it. The will-to-live becomes the will-to-power. Only rarely does nature provide armors of defense which cannot be transmitted into instruments of aggression."

Third, the desire for a comfortable life disposes men to obey a common power. Other things inclining men to obey a common power are fear of death and injury, and desire of knowledge, and desire of peace. This last point is more fully developed in Chapters XIII and XIV.

CHAPTER XII.   OF RELIGION

The "seed of religion" is found in man alone, for it is based on "some peculiar quality" that is not found in other creatures. This quality Hobbes calls curiosity about the causes of the events man sees. Man "observeth how one event hath been produced by another, and remembereth in them antecedence and consequence." But, says Hobbes, there is a limit to what man can know about this chain of events, because his experience is limited.

This limitation produces fear and anxiety in man. He is afraid of the unknown causes, or consequences, of the things he observes. "For being assured that there be causes of all things that have arrived hitherto, or shall arrive hereafter," says Hobbes, "it is impossible for a man . . . not to be in a perpetual solicitude of the time to come."

> **COMMENT:** We see a parallel here to the pursuit of power. As appetite drives man in a mad pursuit of power, which ends only in death, so curiosity drives him in an endless pursuit of remote causes, which ends only in sleep: "So that man, which looks too far before him, in the care of the future time, . . . has no repose, nor pause of his anxiety, but in sleep."

Hence, man is destined to live a restless life; this is his inescapable predicament. In both the pursuit of power and the pursuit of remote causes, the ultimate basis of the predicament is fear—on the one hand, the fear of insecurity which leads man to seek power, and on the other hand, the fear of the unknown which leads him to worship a Supreme Being.

This fear of the unknown ultimately finds a sanctuary in which it seeks to resolve itself. According to Hobbes, this sanctuary is provided, in the absence of true knowledge, in a belief in gods, i.e., as in the pagan gods. But Hobbes always professed to be a true Christian believer, and at this point he strongly asserts his faith by resorting to the Thomistic proof of God's existence through causality. Man, he says, will "plunge himself profoundly in the pursuit of causes; shall at last come to this, that there must be . . . one first mover; that is, a first and eternal cause of all things; which is that which men call by the name of God."

COMMENT: What has been discussed so far only explains the predicament of man in isolation. But in the gloomy vision of Hobbes, this is minor compared to the dilemma of social man. In isolation, man has his own nature to put up with, which is bad enough; in relation to others, there is the strain of hostility and discord. In the following chapter, Hobbes discusses the nature of this new human predicament, which brings us to his political philosophy proper.

CHAPTER XIII. OF THE NATURAL CONDITION OF MANKIND AS CONCERNING THEIR FELICITY, AND MISERY

COMMENT: It is a basic assumption of classical political thought that man is by nature political. As Aristotle said in one of his most frequently quoted epigrams, "Man is a political animal." He meant by that two things: first, that man is gregarious (i.e., he seeks the company of other men); second, that man exists within a definite social hierarchy, so that some rule and others are ruled, some are masters and others are slaves, some are fathers and others are sons—all this being natural. Hobbes rejected both premises, asserting, first, that man is *not* naturally gregarious, but, rather, individualistic; and, second, that men are roughly *equal* by nature. These are the premises upon which he bases what is considered in the field of political philosophy to be the first systematic endeavor to construct a science of politics. This endeavor is brought out in the present chapter. Here Hobbes describes his concept of the "state of nature," a prepolitical (i.e., presocial) condition in which "men live without a common power to keep them all in awe." As Hobbes conceives it, the state of nature amounts to a "state of war."

One thing must be made clear from the beginning, or the student will never arrive at a true understanding of Hobbes. The state of nature is not important as a historical concept. Even Hobbes said at one point, "It may be thought, there was never such a time, nor condition of war as this; and I believe it was never generally so, over all the world. . . ." Still Hobbes tended to believe that something like the condition of war he describes existed at particular times in particular circumstances; for in completing the above-quoted sentence, he says, "but there are many places, where they live so now." But the real value of the state of nature is its use as an analytical device. Hobbes uses it as an aid for his readers. He hopes it will help them to understand certain basic facts of human psychology. Once these facts are understood, the way to an enduring political order, where there is peace, will be made easier. Thus, when we inquire about the state of nature, the real question we are asking is this: "How would human beings act toward one another if they lived in a condition where there is no political organization and discipline?"

Hobbes begins the chapter by asserting that men are roughly equal by nature. They are equal in bodily strength because "the weakest has strength enough to kill the strongest." They are even more equal in mental abilities because these are the result of experience. As to experience, "equal time equally bestows [it] on all men in those things they equally apply themselves unto." It is interesting to note here that Hobbes uses the analogy of "killing" to illustrate his assertion of human equality. This is significant because, as Hobbes tells us time and again, the most fundamental urge of man is "self-preservation" and the greatest of all human passions is the "fear of violent death."

"From equality of ability," Hobbes continues, "arises equality of *hope* in the attaining of our ends," and when any two individuals desire the same thing, which they cannot both enjoy, then they compete with each other and become enemies. The natural psychological outcome of this condition of universal enmity is what Hobbes describes as "diffidence."

COMMENT: The reader is cautioned not to interpret "diffidence" to mean "timidity" or "shyness," i.e., lack of confidence in our own ability. Hobbes' meaning is quite different. What he had in mind was lack of confidence in one's fellow men—in short, "distrust" or "suspicion." This "diffidence" is a natural passion, because in the state of nature no one can rest assured that his neighbors will not at some moment take away his possessions and possibly kill him.

It is bad enough for men to have diffidence in the state of nature. But what makes matters even worse, man is also vain, i.e., he loves "glory." Thus, Hobbes tells us, every man expects that "his companions should value him at the same rate he sets upon himself." And if the companions do not but, rather, undervalue him, then he would seek damage upon his "contemners" so as to "extort a greater value" of himself from them.

With this analysis, Hobbes is now able to list the three "principal causes of quarrel," which are *competition*, *diffidence,* and *glory*. The objects, or goals, of these passions are *gain, safety,* and *reputation,* respectively. These three passions characterize man in the state of nature, so that the state of nature becomes a state of "war of every man against every man." In such a state there is no law, and, consequently, no justice. On the contrary, the two cardinal virtues of men in the state of war are "force and fraud." So it is that the life of man in the state of nature is, in Hobbes' most famous words, "solitary, poor, nasty, brutish, and short." In brief, he is saying that *man is not by nature political,* as Aristotle claimed.

COMMENT: Hobbes' meaning of the term "state of war" demands some clarification. He did not mean actual fighting. Rather, he was speaking of a general atmosphere where "the will to contend by battle is sufficiently known." This may be compared to what Plato termed the "feverish condition." Or it is what we might call today a "cold war."

To use Hobbes' own analogy, the state of war is more like a rainy season than actual rainfall. He says: "For as the nature of foul weather lies not in a shower or two of rain, but in an inclination thereto of many days together, so the nature of war consists not in actual fighting but in the known disposition thereto."

Such is the miserable condition of the state of nature. How do we get out of it? First, says Hobbes, certain *passions* incline us toward peace. These are *fear* of death, *desire* of the things leading to a more commodious life, and the *hope* of obtaining them by hard work. Then, secondly, *reason* "suggests convenient articles of peace upon which men may be drawn to agreement." Hobbes refers to these "articles of peace" as "precepts of reason" or "laws of nature." They are dealt with in the succeeding chapters.

COMMENT: Despite Hobbes' gloomy vision of human nature, he refuses to join the company of theologians in labeling man "wicked" or "depraved." In fact, he never uses a term like "Original Sin." He insists that "the desires and other passions of man are in themselves no sin. No more are the actions that proceed from these passions, till they know a law that forbids them." Without passions man would not even exist, because passions comprise the force that moves him.

Thus, the role of the passions is paramount. It is not the victory of reason over the unruly passions that provides the means of getting out of the state of nature. That would be the case if Hobbes were following the Platonic tradition. But he is not. What actually takes place is this: As a result of bitter experience in the state of nature, certain peace-inclining passions prevail over war-inclining passions. Reason performs only a modest, though crucial, function; it merely "suggests" the best means of gratifying the passions.

CHAPTER XIV. OF THE FIRST AND SECOND NATURAL LAWS, AND OF CONTRACTS

In this chapter Hobbes lays the groundwork for the emergence of men from the state of nature. He first distinguishes the right of nature from a law of nature. The *right of nature* is defined as "the liberty each man has to use his own power, as he will himself, for the preservation of his own nature, that is to say, of his own life." He then defines *liberty* as the "absence of external impediments."

A *law of nature* is a "precept or general rule, found out by reason, by which a man is forbidden to do that which is destructive of his life, or takes away the means of preserving the same, and to omit that by which he thinks it may be best preserved." Thus, a law of nature, like the right of nature, aims at what has been alluded to above as the most fundamental urge of man, i.e., "self-preservation."

The distinction between the two is simply this: right implies liberty, law implies obligation; right is freedom from external impediments, law is an impediment.

> **COMMENT:**   There is a paradox in Hobbes' argument. We have already seen that in the state of nature men have the unlimited right to do all things, including the right to subdue and destroy others. Hobbes defines this natural right as "liberty," which in turn is defined as "absence of external impediments."
>
> Now "absence of external impediments" means ability to act, and this is what we mean by power. This means that natural right is power to do all things—which is absurd, for in the state of nature all men are equal. How is it possible that all men simultaneously enjoy absolute power to do all things? The answer is that it is not possible, because, as Hobbes himself says, all men are roughly equal in power, and they act as a check upon one another.

Hobbes never equates right with might, as Spinoza and others did after him. And yet, that is what follows from his definition of natural right as liberty to do all things. The equation of might with right is not in itself a contradiction, except for the fact that it is not consistent with Hobbes' description of the state of nature.

Hobbes' fundamental error lies in his attempt to positivistically define "right," that is, to define it as if it were a fact. But it is not a fact; it is a value. That I have a life, or that I live, is a fact; that I have a "right" to life is an assertion. In defining right as liberty, and liberty as the absence of impediments, he is treating it, wrongly, as if it were a fact. At any rate, men must somehow avoid the perils to their existence that inevitably follow from the exercise of their natural right. Thanks to the good office of *reason,* which has prescribed the "articles of peace," men have now found ways of preserving themselves by following the *laws of nature.*

The first and fundamental law of nature enjoins men "to endeavor peace, as far as he has hope of obtaining it." But lest we forget the ultimate purpose of this, which is self-preservation, Hobbes hastens to add that "when he cannot obtain it . . . he may seek and use all helps and advantages of war."

The second law of nature is a corollary of the first, in that it tells us how we should go about endeavoring peace: "That a man be willing, when others are so too, as far-forth as for peace and defence of himself he shall think it necessary, to lay down this right to all things; and be contented with so much liberty against other men, as he would allow other men against himself."

COMMENT: The expression "laying down" requires some explanation. By that Hobbes did not mean that people actually surrender their rights in such a manner that someone else might "pick them up." All Hobbes means is that they stop exercising their own right and in the meantime refrain from "hindering another of the benefit of his own right." This is done by simply "standing out of his way." We can see that anyone who is allowed to "enjoy his own original right" alone is in fact enjoying an absolute power over the rest. This is so because his natural right, which in the state of nature was only potentially absolute, has now become actually absolute—by virtue of having been made free of others' obstruction.

A right may be laid down either by simply renouncing it with no beneficiary in view, or by transferring it to someone else, whereby a definite party is designated as the recipient, or beneficiary. For Hobbes, the appropriate method is *transfer*. A mutually agreed transfer of right is what we mean by *contract*. Civil society is created by the *social contract,* wherein *each man together with every other man transfers his right to a beneficiary, who is not himself a party to the contract* and obliges himself not to resist the commands of the latter.

Now, transfer or renunciation of one's right is a purely voluntary act, and as such the object is some good to himself—above all, his security and bodily preservation. Consequently, there are some rights, Hobbes tells us, which no one can be presumed to have abandoned or transferred, and the loss of which would defeat the original purpose of the contract. For example, no one can be regarded as having laid down his right to resist anyone who attempts to take away his life, "because he cannot be understood to aim thereby at any good to himself."

COMMENT: Later on, Hobbes says with a touch of irony: "Though a man may covenant thus, 'Unless I do so, or so, kill me,' he cannot covenant thus, 'Unless I do so, or so, I will not resist you, when you come to kill me.' For man by nature chooses the lesser evil, which is danger of death in resisting; rather than the greater, which is certain and present death in not resisting."

It is clear that Hobbes is here deliberately creating a tension between (1) the absolute right of the sovereign (his natural right to do anything, which he retains by virtue of having been outside the contract), and (2) the citizen's basic right of self-defense, which he has not renounced when entering into the contract. Hobbes reiterates this argument in Chapter XXI with greater clarity.

In a contract there are two stages: *covenant*, which is an exchange of promises, and actual *performance*. Covenant, then, implies a *trust* and presupposes a minimum degree of fidelity, or faith, on the part of the respective parties making it. But what use is it if it is but a promise for a future act and not a present performance? Obviously, none. What is crucial to a contract, then, is the enforcement of the covenant.

So it is that a covenant is valid only when there is a *common power* set over all the parties "with right and force sufficient to compel performance." In short, there is no valid covenant where there is a reasonable fear on the part of each of nonperformance by the other. Thus, says Hobbes, without the "fear of some common coercive power" the parties are no better off than they are in the state of nature. One would only "betray himself to his enemy" if he were to perform his obligation first and accept at face value the others' promise to live up to their part of the bargain. He would only be giving up his right without getting anything in return, "because the bonds of words are too weak to bridle men's ambition, avarice, anger, and other passions, without the fear of some coercive power."

There must always be penalties for nonfulfillment, because "bonds . . . have their strength not from their own nature, for nothing is more easily broken than a man's word, but from fear of some evil consequence upon the rupture." It is then the proper function of government to see to it that the terror of punishment be greater than the benefit one may expect from breach of covenant (Chapter XV).

CHAPTER XV. OF OTHER LAWS OF NATURE

The third law of nature is that men must perform their covenants; if they do not do so they remain in a condition of war. Thus, "injustice" is defined as not performing a covenant. Covenants of mutual trust are invalid when there is a fear of nonperformance on either side; therefore, the validity of covenants begins with the constitution of the civil power, as does "propriety" itself.

Sixteen more "laws of nature" are listed, which include gratitude, complaisance (by which Hobbes means mutual accommodation, or sociability), plus injunctions against cruelty, pride, arrogance, etc.

The laws of nature may be summed up by the following rule, a negative statement of the Golden Rule: "Do not that to another, which thou wouldest not have done to thyself." If a man accepts this as his rule of behavior, "then there is none of these laws of nature that will not appear unto him very reasonable." The laws of nature are "immutable and eternal."

The chapter concludes with an attempt by Hobbes to clarify what he means by the terms "law" and "laws of nature." "These dictates of reason, men used to call by the name of laws, but improperly: for they are but conclusions, or theorems concerning what conduceth to the conservation and defense of themselves; whereas law, properly, is the word of him, that by right hath command over others." That is, these "laws" are theorems until they are actually commanded by a civil sovereign, at which time they become laws in the full sense of the term as Hobbes uses it. "But yet if we consider the same theorems, as delivered in the word of God," he continues, "that by right commandeth all things; then are they properly called laws." That is, to the man who believes in God, the laws of nature are laws and not theorems even before they are promulgated by the civil sovereign.

CHAPTER XVI. OF PERSONS, AUTHORS, AND THINGS PERSONATED

This chapter lays the semantic groundwork for the appearance of the great *Leviathan*. First, a *person* is defined as he "whose words or actions are considered either as his own, or as representing the words or actions of another man." If his words or actions are his own, he is a *natural person;* if they represent someone else, he is an *artificial person.*

The person whose words or actions are represented by the artificial person is said to be the *author;* and the artificial person is said to speak with *authority.* In the sense that the artificial person represents the words and actions of the author, he may also be called the *actor.*

A commonwealth, or state, is an artificial man (Introduction to *Leviathan*). In this instance, "a multitude of men are made *one* person," for they are represented by one person. This is so because what makes the person one is not the unity of the represented, but "the unity of the representer." However, "if the representative consists of many men" (as in a democracy), says Hobbes, "the voice of the greater number must be considered as the voice of them all."

> **COMMENT:** This chapter is not a mere exercise in semantics. Its real significance lies in the fact that, inasmuch as the sovereign is originally chosen by the people, whatever he does is justified, for he is merely "representing" the people's words and actions.
>
> The full force of the argument will emerge in Chapter XVIII, where Hobbes was now able to say: since "every particular man is author of all the sovereign doth . . . , he that complaineth of injury from his sovereign, complaineth of that whereof he himself is author; and therefore ought not to accuse any man but himself."

PART II.   OF COMMONWEALTH

CHAPTER XVII.   OF THE CAUSES, GENERATION, AND DEFINITION OF A COMMONWEALTH

In the opening paragraphs of this chapter, Hobbes summarizes the main arguments of the last few chapters of Part I. His purpose is to explain the end of commonwealth. The "final cause, end, or design" of men in imposing upon themselves a political discipline is, says Hobbes, men's foresight of their own preservation and a more comfortable life.

This involves the creation of a visible power "to keep them in awe and tie them by fear of punishment to the performance of their covenants." In other words, what is needed to make the covenant good is the power to enforce it; *authority* and *power* must reside in one hand, for "covenants without the sword are but words."

Why is it that men with their gift of reason and language cannot live together harmoniously without a common police power above them? How do men compare with ants and bees, who also lead a collective life? Hobbes' answer is simple and clear: these lower forms of animal live together by their natural instinct of sociability, whereas men are drawn together only through an artificial arrangement called "contract." In short, men are by nature antisocial.

How does Hobbes arrive at this conclusion? He notes, for one thing, that men, unlike the simpler creatures, are continually in competition with one another for honor and dignity. Consequently the lives of men are marked by hatred and envy. In addition, Hobbes finds that the world of the lower social animals holds no distinction between "common good" and "private good," whereas the world of human beings is characterized by a perennial tension between the two spheres. This tension is only natural, Hobbes tells us, because man's joy consists in a sense of eminence, which one attains through comparing himself with his fellow men. In this situation, one cannot attain his private goals except at the expense of the public's goals.

> **COMMENT:**   The argument that man's sociability, or "agreement," is not natural, but "by covenant only"—i.e., purely artificial, is an important element in Hobbes' political thought. For here again we find his radical break with the Aristotelian-Thomistic tradition. (See comments to Chapter XIII.)
>
> By *nature,* man is, so to speak, condemned to be miserable. For even the peace-inclining *passions* (Chapter XIII) are dormant insofar as they are incapable of self-guidance. It is through the exercise of his *reason,* which is not born with him but attained only by industry (Chapter V), that he is redeemed (Chapter XIII). This redemption comes about through the *convention* of "social contract," which means making covenant one with another to institute a common sovereign power (Chapter XIV).

The only way to erect such a common power, according to Hobbes, is to confer the power of all men upon one man, or assembly of men, "that may reduce all their wills by plurality of voices, into one will." This is the artificial will of the office of the sovereign, who impersonates the men making the covenant. When this power is so conferred, each man will "acknowledge himself to be author of whatsoever he that so beareth their [*sic*] person shall act, or cause to be acted, in those things which concern the common peace and safety; and therein to submit their wills, every one to his will, and their judgments, to his judgment."

The artificial person so created is a *sovereign,* and those who created him, i.e., the "authors" of this artifact, are his *subjects.* This multitude of men so arranged is collectively called a *commonwealth,* or *civitas* (civil society). And this is the generation of the great *Leviathan,* "or rather, to speak more reverently, of that *mortal god,* to which we owe under the *immortal God,* our peace and defense."

A sovereign power may come into being in two ways: (1) by force (which produces a "commonwealth by acquisition"), and (2) through voluntary agreement, or covenant, among men (which produces a "commonwealth by institution").

CHAPTER XVIII.   OF THE RIGHTS OF SOVEREIGNS BY INSTITUTION

In this important chapter Hobbes defends the principle of absolute sovereignty. He proceeds, first, by establishing a popular source for the sovereign power. The sovereign power, he says, "is conferred by the consent of the people assembled." All this is perfectly consistent with what has already been said by Hobbes in Chapter XIV and XVI.

Hobbes now makes a curious distinction between the creation of a commonwealth and the selection of a sovereign. The creation of a commonwealth was discussed in the last chapter: the covenant of every man with every other man—which means that there is no minority, i.e., no dissenter, since those refusing to covenant will simply be left in the state of nature by their own choosing.

However, this covenant-making does not extend to the selection of the sovereign person (person in this case meaning one man or an assembly). In a sense, the covenant is no more than making a promise to obey at some time in the future whichever sovereign person the majority may choose. Hobbes refers twice in this chapter to those who have made their covenant but have not yet chosen their sovereign as members of a "congregation." Once the majority of the congregation has decided on whom to entrust the sovereign power, says Hobbes, "every one, as well he that voted for it, as he that voted against it, shall authorize all the actions and judgments of that man, or assembly of men, in the same manner, as if they were his own." Later in the same chapter Hobbes discusses the need for majority rule in the choice of a sovereign person: "For if he voluntarily entered into the congregation of them that were assembled, he sufficiently declared thereby his will, and therefore tacitly covenanted, to stand to what the major part should ordain."

COMMENT: This distinction between a covenant-making and the choosing of a sovereign has generally been dismissed by commentators as being inconsequential to Hobbes' basic arguments. First of all, this distinction is clearly in conflict with Hobbes' original definition of social contract, in which the covenant-making at the same time involves the selection of a sovereign (see Chapter XIV). Secondly, it is not a profoundly significant distinction, for Hobbes never seeks to justify revolution on the basis of it. Locke, however, who makes this same distinction, does precisely this. He distinguishes between a "civil society" (the product of a contract) and a "government" (the product of a trust by that society). Because the government is merely a trust of the society, the government may be overthrown by the latter.

In any event, one should at least take cognizance of the fact that, as in Locke so in Hobbes—in this particular chapter—the choice of a particular government is made not by mutual covenant of everyone with everyone, but only by the majority of the congregation. The congregation was already established by covenant, and through the covenant agreed to abide by the will of the majority.

Whatever the means of selecting the sovereign person, the absolute character of his power and authority is what Hobbes is truly interested in defending. Following are some of the consequences of the institution of sovereign power.

The subjects cannot change the form of government. "They that have already instituted a commonwealth, being thereby bound by covenant, to own the actions, and judgments of one," Hobbes argues, "cannot lawfully make a new covenant, against themselves, to be obedient to any other, in anything whatsoever, without his permission."

Rebellion becomes indefensible, a contradiction in terms. Hobbes' argument here is a logical deduction from his doctrine of impersonation found in Chapter XVI. "Besides," says Hobbes, "if he that attempteth to depose his sovereign be killed, or punished by him for such attempt, he is author of his own punishment, as being by the institution, author of all his sovereign shall do." Hobbes goes on to demolish the argument of divine justification of civil disobedience: "And whereas some men have pretended for their disobedience to their sovereign, a new covenant, made not with men, but with God; this also is unjust: for there is no covenant with God, but by mediation of somebody that representeth God's person; which none but God's lieutenant, who hath sovereignty under God."

> COMMENT: Over a century later, Jean Jacques Rousseau, who was on the whole very critical of Hobbes' ideas, had this to say about the latter's insistence upon the subordination of the church to the authority of the state: "Of all Christian writers, the philosopher Hobbes alone has seen the evil and how to remedy it, and has dared to propose the reunion of the two heads of the eagle, and the restoration throughout of political unity. . . ."

No subject can, by any pretense of forfeiture, be freed from his subjection, because there can be no breach of covenant on the part of the sovereign. This is so, says Hobbes, because the sovereign power was entrusted to him through a "covenant only of one [subject] to another, and not of him [the sovereign] to any of them [the subjects]."

> COMMENT: In other words, the sovereign power must be absolute, because it is not bound by any covenant. This is so because the sovereign was outside the covenant. The sovereign makes no covenant with his subjects beforehand,

because men do not exist as a group before the establishment of the sovereign power. They exist only as separate individuals, and they become a collective person only through the sovereign whom they have set up over themselves. They establish the sovereign only as separate individuals, and are therefore incapable of making a covenant with the sovereign in advance.

In opposition to the theory of limited sovereignty, Hobbes has this to say: "The opinion that any monarch receiveth his power by covenant, that is to say, on condition, proceedeth from want of understanding of this easy truth, that covenants being but words and breath, have no force to oblige, contain, constrain, or protect any man, but what it has from the public sword." For Hobbes, then, the sovereign power is absolute and unconditional.

The sovereign may commit *iniquity*, but not *injustice* or *injury*. Injustice has been defined as the nonperformance of covenant, and injury as the condition resulting from such nonperformance. Since the sovereign is not a party to the covenant, he is not bound by its terms, as are his subjects. Thus he cannot commit either injustice or injury resulting from nonperformance of it. It also follows that the sovereign can never be justly punished, "for seeing every subject is author of the actions of his sovereign; he punisheth another for the actions committed by himself."

The sovereign is judge of what doctrines are fit to be taught to his subjects. Hobbes, perhaps more than any other major thinker up to his time, was deeply conscious of the ideological causes of political disorder. For him, the key to political redemption was the right kind of political philosophy, such as his own (see Chapter XXXI). He thought that the causes of political dissolution could be attributed to the prevalence of wrong opinions about the origin and purpose of government. Because, Hobbes thought, "the actions of men proceed from their opinions," he was willing to go to the extent of imposing strict censorship "as a thing necessary to peace; thereby to prevent discord and civil war."

The sovereign regulates property. Before the creation of the sovereign power, all men had the right to all things, which was one cause of war in the state of nature. Therefore, these rules of "mine and thine," good and evil, lawful and unlawful, in short, the civil laws, are basic to peace and basic to sovereign power. The sovereign also decides controversies. If he did not the civil laws would be in vain, and there would be no difference between a commonwealth and the state of nature.

Other rights of the sovereign include making war and peace, choosing his councilors and ministers, making rewards and punishments, and giving titles of honor and order.

"These are the rights," says Hobbes, "which make the essence of sovereignty." They are inseparable and indivisible from the sovereign, for "a kingdom divided in itself cannot stand." Hobbes cites the English civil war, through which he lived, to illustrate this point.

In summing up this remarkable chapter in defense of absolute sovereignty, Hobbes writes as follows: "But a man may here object, that the condition of subjects is very miserable; as being obnoxious to the lusts and other irregular passions of him, or them that have so unlimited a power in their hands." But anyone who so objects, says Hobbes, is "not considering that the state of man can never be without some incommodity or other; and that the greatest, that in any form of government can possibly happen to the people in general, is scarce sensible in respect of the miseries, and horrible calamities, that accompany a civil war, or that dissolute condition of masterless men, without subjection to laws, and a coercive power to tie their hands from rapine and revenge. . . . For all men are by nature provided of notable multiplying glasses, that is their passions and self-love, through which, every little payment appeareth a great grievance; but are destitute of those prospective glasses, namely moral and civil science, to see afar off the miseries that hang over them, and cannot without such payments be avoided."

CHAPTER XIX. OF THE SEVERAL KINDS OF COMMONWEALTH BY INSTITUTION, AND OF SUCCESSION TO THE SOVEREIGN POWER

In this chapter, Hobbes elaborates on the previous discussion. He identifies three kinds of commonwealth by institution—*monarchy,* in which the sovereignty is in one man; *democracy,* an assembly of all the people; and *aristocracy,* an assembly of a part. These divisions are simple enough. They are found in political philosophers from Plato onward. Hobbes, however, will recognize no other forms, as do Plato and Aristotle. Tyranny, oligarchy, and anarchy, says Hobbes, are merely monarchy, aristocracy, and democracy "misliked."

It is important to note that the difference in the three forms does not consist in a difference of power. For the sovereign power is always the same, no matter what the form of government. Rather, the difference lies in the "difference of convenience or aptitude to produce peace and security." In other words, peace and security are the main objectives of commonwealth. The three forms—monarchy, aristocracy, and democracy—are merely three different ways of achieving this end. Whichever form a particular commonwealth chooses is a matter of convenience.

This does not mean Hobbes does not like one form better than the others. He has a clear preference for monarchy. And he spends a good part of this chapter setting forth his reasons why. Hobbes argues that the public interest is advanced most where the public and private interests of the sovereign are most closely united. Remember that a sovereign, no matter what the form of commonwealth, is human, whether the sovereign be one or many. As political leader and human being all in one, the sovereign is both public and private person (or persons). So he has (or they have) both public and private interests. Hobbes says that these interests are best united in a monarch.

He adduces several reasons for this. Among them we may discern one broad principle upon which all are based. And this is that the monarch, being one person, represents the greatest possible unity of sovereign power. It is true enough, says Hobbes, that the monarch has all the weaknesses of human nature. The monarch may be corrupt, indulge in nepotism, play favorites. But the members of an assembly have this same weakness, plus the added weakness of numbers, which makes them disunited. And to Hobbes nothing could be worse than disunity.

Finally, Hobbes takes up in this chapter the question of succession. This is an important issue for political theory. One crucial flaw of dictatorship in modern times is usually the failure to provide for the orderly transfer of power upon the death of the dictator. This often results in a violent struggle for power, conditions of chaos, and great hardships for the people. Hobbes' discussion of succession is sadly outdated, and bears little relevance to our modern problem. He bases it on what he asserts to be the sovereign's right to transfer the sovereign power to whomever he wishes to succeed him after death. He reasons that once sovereignty is given, it remains forever with him to whom it was given. Therefore, the sovereign may dispose of it as he wishes.

> **COMMENT:**   Hobbes' reasoning in this case seems not to be based on "natural" principles, but rather on custom as it prevailed up to that time—specifically, on the custom of primogeniture (succession of the first-born son).
>
> Moreover, there is a paradox in Hobbes' treatment of democracy as a form of sovereignty. We have seen that the sovereign is such by virtue of unlimited, indivisible, unconditional—in short, absolute—power. The sovereign power is absolute because the sovereign is not bound by any covenant, being outside the contract.
>
> But herein lies the paradox. How can the whole people become their own sovereign? If they were to do so, they would have to remain outside the contract. But if the whole people must stay out of the contract in order to be-

come sovereign, that is, absolute sovereign, who is to make the covenant? Hobbes does not provide an answer.

CHAPTER XX. OF DOMINION PATERNAL AND DESPOTICAL

Previously, Hobbes spoke of two kinds of commonwealth— commonwealth by institution, and commonwealth by acquisition. We have considered the first. We shall now briefly consider the second. First, however, it should be noted that the difference between the two is one of degree rather than of kind. In either case the motive for entering into commonwealth is *fear*. In the case of institution, men give sovereignty out of fear for each other. In the case of acquisition, men give sovereignty out of fear of him to whom it is given.

There are two kinds of dominion, or commonwealth by acquisition. These are paternal dominion and dominion by conquest. Paternal dominion comes about naturally through generation. Dominion by conquest comes about exactly as the term implies —by conquest.

Here again, there is a single underlying principle that unites the two kinds of dominion, and, in fact, unites dominion generally with commonwealth by institution. This is the covenant. For example, the parents' right of sovereignty over their children, says Hobbes, derives not from the fact of procreation, but from the consent of the children. This consent may not be, and probably would not be, expressed by the children. But it is at least implied by the very fact that the children remain under the protection of the parents. In other words, the children give tacit consent.

This explains why it is that within the household the father is the sovereign power. He is the strongest person and the protector. If sovereignty were derived from generation, the mother would be sovereign, because it is she who actually produces the children.

The same principle of consent holds for dominion by conquest. "It is . . . not the victory that giveth the right of dominion over the vanquished," says Hobbes, "but his own covenant."

CHAPTER XXI.   OF THE LIBERTY OF SUBJECTS

COMMENT: So much for the types of commonwealth. What of the subjects who live in a commonwealth? What liberties do they have as members of a commonwealth? Remember that in the state of nature, men had absolute liberty to do whatever they liked, so long as they could get away with it. In entering a commonwealth they agreed to give up their right to all things, and put themselves under the protection of a sovereign who was to assure their peace and security. Do the subjects of a commonwealth retain any of their natural rights? This is the question that occupies Hobbes in the present chapter.

The answer to the question is strongly suggested by the very definition of the term "liberty." Liberty, says Hobbes, "is the absence of opposition, or external impediment." To put it in human terms, a person is free who does what he wills (or does not what he wills not). One could even do something out of fear or necessity, and it would still be an act of free will. "Fear and liberty," says Hobbes, "are consistent."

Men, acting out of fear, freely enter into a commonwealth, and thereby give up, as has been said, their absolute freedom and accept restrictions. These restrictions in a commonwealth (these external impediments) are the civil laws given by the sovereign. And since it is the sovereign who gives the civil laws (and thus applies external impediments), the liberty of subjects lies in those things permitted by the sovereign. To quote Hobbes, "The liberty of a subject, lieth therefore only in those things, which in regulating their actions, the sovereign hath pretermitted. . . ." (Pretermit means to omit, let pass, or to leave untouched.) Later on in the chapter, Hobbes states the matter very clearly: "In cases where the sovereign has prescribed no rule, there the subject hath the liberty to do, or forbear, according to his own discretion." These liberties of the subject lie outside the public sphere—as, for example, in contracts, choice of home, diet, rearing children, etc. Such liberties depend upon "the silence of the law."

However, there is one very important exception to this notion of liberty of subjects. The basic goal of men is always security, whether in the state of nature or in a commonwealth. Indeed, this is the reason for entering the commonwealth. Therefore, the sovereign cannot expect his subjects to give up their basic right of self-defense. This means he cannot command them to kill themselves or to accuse themselves in a way that will result in their death. This does not prevent the sovereign from asking subjects to face death in battle for the common defense. It would mean, to draw a specific illustration, that the sovereign could not take one of his subjects aside, hand him a knife, say to him, "kill yourself," *and expect him to do it*. The subject would be justified in turning the knife on the sovereign if he thought that was the only way to preserve himself.

COMMENT: The reader is reminded, for instance, of what Hobbes said in Chapter XIV: "For though a man may covenant thus, 'Unless I do so or so, kill me,' he cannot covenant thus, 'Unless I do so, or so, I will not resist you, when you come to kill me.' For man by nature chooseth the lesser evil, which is danger of death in resisting; rather than the greater, which is certain and present death in not resisting."

This eternal freedom of self-defense Hobbes calls "the true liberty of subjects." And in it lies the seed of revolution, or what Hobbes himself termed "the liberty to disobey."

CHAPTER XXII. OF SYSTEMS SUBJECT, POLITICAL, AND PRIVATE

It does not take a philosopher to observe that within a common-wealth (or within a society, as we would say) there exist lesser groups. A society is not simply a conglomeration of individuals in a single monolithic organization; the individuals also join smaller organizations as their interests or business dictate.

Hobbes devotes this chapter to a discussion of these smaller groups, or "systems," as he calls them. The discussion is of no great value, and adds little or nothing to what has already been said. Suffice it to say that membership in a smaller group in no way reduces the obligation of the subject to obey the sovereign. Loyalty to the commonwealth transcends private interest.

CHAPTER XXIII. OF THE PUBLIC MINISTERS OF SOVEREIGN POWER

Hobbes continues his piece-by-piece examination of the commonwealth by focusing here on public ministers employed in the affairs of the commonwealth. Once again there is little of significance. It is perhaps worth mentioning that the public minister, according to Hobbes, is really two persons, a natural private human being and a politician serving the public. Also, the fact that he is a minister means that he serves by authority of the sovereign.

CHAPTER XXIV. OF THE NUTRITION, AND PROCREATION OF A COMMONWEALTH

COMMENT: In Hobbes' time great thinkers spread themselves around more than they do today. The frontiers of knowledge were not so vast, and the division of subject matter did not exist to anywhere near the extent that it does now. So it was that Hobbes traversed a greater number of academic fields than any modern academician would dare. He delved into psychology, politics, administration, the law, economics, theology, and even mathematics—all this in addition to what today we call "philosophy."

In this chapter Hobbes discusses some problems of economics. We know economics today as a subject of great complexity, and, in retrospect, Hobbes' discussion of it seems rudimentary. However, it contains some insights which later thinkers, such as Locke, the Utilitarians, and Karl Marx, were to develop into famous themes. For example, after defining commodities in general as natural and manufactured goods, and therefore exchangeable, Hobbes points out that labor itself is a commodity, and also exchangeable. This means that a person, as a commodity, markets himself. He sells himself for whatever price the demand for his skill will bring.

> **COMMENT:**   The notion of labor as a commodity is undoubtedly an advance over that of slave labor, but it appears to be only a stepping stone to an even broader conception of labor as creative human endeavor.

Hobbes lived in turbulent times, when great issues divided men in stern and sometimes violent opposition to one another. One of the issues was property. Hobbes took a position that property is an effect of commonwealth, i.e., it exists through civil laws given by the sovereign. A landowner had the right to exclude all subjects of the commonwealth from his property, but not the sovereign.

> **COMMENT:**   The seeds of socialism are contained in this proposition. Although Hobbes was no socialist in the modern sense of the word, it is certainly no great leap from the notion that property exists by virtue of the laws given by the sovereign to the right of government ownership.

A generation or two later, Locke was to take a position on the issue of property in direct opposition to that of Hobbes.

He was to say that property was natural, and, therefore, that it was the responsibility of government to preserve it for the individual members of society.

CHAPTER XXV.   OF COUNSEL

This chapter is valuable more as groundwork for the next than in itself. The important concept to understand is *"command."* We shall see why in the next chapter. When one commands, Hobbes tells us, he says, "Do this," or "Do not that," and expects that the order will be carried out. A command is given for the benefit of the person doing the commanding.

Command is to be contrasted to *counsel*. When one counsels, he says, "Do this," or "Do not that," without expecting that his counsel will necessarily be carried out. And he does so for the benefit of the person to whom the counsel is given. A command carries an obligation to obey; counsel does not.

CHAPTER XXVI.   OF CIVIL LAWS

Law is a command, not a command of just any man to any man, "but only of him, whose command is addressed to one formerly obliged to obey him."

Civil law is distinguished from other laws in that it indicates the name of the person commanding, which is *"persona civitatis,"* or the person of the commonwealth. Following is Hobbes' definition: "Civil law," he says, "is to every subject those rules which the commonwealth hath commanded him, by word, writing, or other sufficient sign of the will, to make use of for the distinction of right and wrong; that is to say, of what is contrary and what is not contrary to the rule."

The maker of laws is called the *legislator;* and in all commonwealths, the legislator alone is the sovereign, or, conversely, "the sovereign is the sole legislator." And since the sovereign is identical with the legislator, the latter can be one man or many, depending on the type of commonwealth.

Consistent with his theory of absolute sovereignty, Hobbes argues that the sovereign is not subject to his own laws, "for having power to make and repeal laws, he may when he pleaseth, free himself from that subjection, by repealing those laws that trouble him, and making of new." This is so, says Hobbes, because it is impossible "for any person to be bound to himself." But Hobbes is silent as to whether or not a sovereign may ignore or violate the laws (even though they are his) while they are in force, that is to say, without first repealing them.

When Hobbes says that law is a command, he means to emphasize that it is an expression of *will,* not of tradition or custom. It is will that gives a law its positive quality. This is why Hobbes looks upon both human and divine law as "positive." Both emanate from wills, one from divine will, the other from human will.

Now civil laws gain their force from the will of the sovereign. Thus, even if custom should obtain the force of law, it does so because the sovereign permits it by his silence, "for silence is sometimes an agreement of consent," and not just because it is custom.

> **COMMENT:** By this view of custom, Hobbes is taking issue with the whole tradition of English common law, which is England's major contribution to the field of jurisprudence. The common law has its origin in men's adherence to custom as the source of legitimacy. The common law is unwritten, and is based on precedents set by previous judicial decision. It is distinguished from Roman and canon laws, which are contained strictly in written statutes.
>
> Hobbes expressed his disapproval of common law as early as Chapter XI. "Ignorance of the causes and original constitution of right, equity, law, and justice," he says, "dis-

poseth a man to make custom and example the rule of his actions; in such manner as to think that unjust which it hath been the custom to punish; and that just, of the impunity and approbation whereof they can produce an example or (as the lawyers which only use this false measure of justice barbarously call it) a precedent; like little children that have no other rule of good and evil manners but the correction they receive from their parents and masters. . . ."

That should make it clear enough, and emphatic enough, that for Hobbes the quality of civil law is not to be determined by its age. Instead, one should consider whether the law is "reasonable." All customs erroneously labeled "law" must first be measured against this yardstick. And if it is truly found to be erroneous law, i.e., unreasonable, it must be abolished. Now Hobbes finds it opportune to reassert his doctrine of absolute sovereignty. He tells us that "the judgment of what is reasonable, of what is to be abolished, belongeth to him that maketh the law, which is the sovereign assembly or monarch."

Inasmuch as civil laws must be reasonable and inasmuch as reasonableness is the attribute of the law of nature, "the law of nature and the civil law contain each other, and are of equal extent." Justice means performance of covenant and giving to every man his due. This is a law of nature, and it is the natural law which makes the civil law meaningful. On the other hand, the natural laws are "not properly laws, but qualities that dispose men to peace and obedience." It is only when the sovereign commands these dictates of nature that they become "civil laws."

In this sense, "the law of nature . . . is a part of the civil law in all commonwealths of the world. Reciprocally also, the civil law is a part of the dictates of nature." Hobbes goes on to say that "civil and natural law are not different kinds, but different parts of law; whereof one part being written, is called civil and the other unwritten, natural."

CHAPTER XXVII. OF CRIMES, EXCUSES, AND EXTENUATIONS

Just as law had its origin in the state of nature, so does crime. Crime originates in sin. Hobbes declares that "a sin is not only a transgression of a law, but also any contempt of the legislator." This is because "such contempt is a breach of all his laws at once."

A sin consists not only in the *commission* of what is forbidden by the laws or the *omission* of what the law commands, but also in the "*intention*, or purpose, to transgress." This follows logically because the intention to break the law is a form of contempt of the legislator, which in itself is a sin.

Now Hobbes turns to crime and its relation to sin. He defines crime as "a sin consisting in the committing, by deed or word, of that which the law forbiddeth, or the omission of what it hath commanded." It follows that *every crime is a sin,* even though *not every sin is a crime.*

Thus, "violation of covenants, ingratitudes, arrogance, and all facts contrary to any moral virtue, can never cease to be sin," because the natural law is eternal. However, commission or omission of the dictates and injunctions of these natural laws are not crimes unless and until they are so declared by the civil law. Consequently, "the civil law ceasing, crimes cease; for there being no other law remaining, but that of nature, there is no place for accusation; every man being his own judge, and accused only by his own conscience, and cleared by the uprightness of his own intention." This is but another way of saying that "when the sovereign power ceaseth, crime also ceaseth, for where there is no such power, there is no protection to be had from the law."

According to Hobbes, "The source of every crime is some defect of the understanding, or some error in reasoning, or some sudden force of the passions." Defect in the understanding is *ignorance;* in reasoning, *erroneous opinion.* Hobbes lists three kinds of ignorance: ignorance of the law, of the sovereign, and of the penalty. Likewise, there are three kinds of erroneous opinion: the presumption of false principles (e.g., "that justice is but a vain word; that whatsoever a man can get by his own industry and hazard is his own"; or that "examples of former times are good arguments of doing the like again"), misinterpretation of the laws of nature by false teachers, and false inferences from true principles by the same.

As for ignorance, Hobbes says that in some cases it is excusable and in others inexcusable. For example, "ignorance of the law of nature excuseth no man; because every man that hath attained to the use of reason is supposed to know he ought not to do to another what he would not have done to himself." However, says Hobbes, when a man goes to a strange land, his ignorance of the civil law of that country should "excuse" him "till it be declared to him; because till then no civil law is binding." Likewise—and this is an important argument—"if the civil law of a man's own country be not so sufficiently declared . . . the ignorance is a good excuse."

One of the passions that most frequently causes crime is *vainglory,* which is the overrating of oneself. Hate, lust, ambition, covetousness, and other passions also cause men to commit crime. But there is also a passion which inclines men not to break the law. This is fear. Fear, says Hobbes, is "the only thing, when there is appearance of profit or pleasure by breaking the laws, that makes men keep them." This is precisely why, as we have noted in Chapter XV, we must create a system of perpetual terror—"terror of some punishment greater than the benefit they expect by the breach of their covenant."

The rest of this chapter is devoted to an examination of the "degrees of crime," which Hobbes believed could be measured by the following four criteria: (1) the malignity of the source, or cause, (2) the contagion of the example, (3) the mischief of the effect, and (4) the concurrence of the times, places, and persons.

> **COMMENT:** This is a strikingly modern and humane conception of crime. Up to Hobbes' time, and even after, different circumstances, degrees, and implications of diverse crimes had rarely been given their due consideration in convicting a criminal. Here, Hobbes is endeavoring to correct this old and "unreasonable" custom (see comments to Chapter XVI).
>
> For instance, Hobbes would say that "a crime arising from a sudden passion is not so great as when the same ariseth from long meditation." This anticipates a distinction we now make in our courts between first-degree murder and second- or third-degree murder. If Hobbes had been in the position of the captain in Herman Melville's classic story "Billy Budd," he would probably not have sentenced Billy to death for his unpremeditated and unintended murder of his arrogant superior on the deck.

CHAPTER XXVIII.   OF PUNISHMENTS AND REWARDS

Hobbes defines punishment as evil inflicted by public authority for what is judged by the public authority to be a crime. The purpose of punishment is to better dispose men to obedience.

Where does the sovereign get his right of punishment? According to what Hobbes has already said, it cannot come from any concession on the part of the subject. If it did, the subject would be laying down his right of self-preservation, which he can never surrender. In Chapter XIV, Hobbes writes, "No man can transfer, or lay down, his right to save himself from death, wounds, and imprisonment." Now he adds that "in the making of a commonwealth, every man giveth away the right of defending another; but not of defending himself. Also he obligeth himself to assist him that hath the sovereignty, in punishing of another; but of himself not." Clearly then, the sovereign's right of punishment must come from some other source.

Hobbes says it comes from the natural right of the sovereign to punish, which is strengthened by the fact that in entering into commonwealth the subjects laid down their own natural right to punish ("so that it was not given, but left to him, and to him only"). The sovereign's right to punish is limited only by the law of nature.

Hobbes draws a number of inferences from this definition of punishment. Among them are the following: Private revenge is not punishment because it does not have behind it the force of public authority. Punishment requires that the act be first judged to be a crime. It also requires that the punishment be aimed at disposing the criminal to obedience to the law. The harm inflicted in punishment must be greater than the benefit derived from the crime (otherwise the apparent good of the criminal act will outweigh the evil of the punishment). The sovereign or his representative may not be punished.

CHAPTER XXIX.   OF THOSE THINGS THAT WEAKEN, OR TEND TO THE DISSOLUTION OF A COMMONWEALTH

COMMENT: In Chapter XVII, Hobbes used the term "mortal god" to "reverently" describe the Leviathan. And in Chapter XXI he makes it clear that a commonwealth must be mortal: "And though sovereignty, in the intention of them that make it, be immortal; yet it is in its own nature, not only subject to violent death, by foreign war; but also through the ignorance, and passions of men, it hath in it, from the very institution, many seeds of a natural mortality, by intestine discord."

In the present chapter, however, Hobbes sounds a note of optimism: "Though nothing can be immortal, which mortals make; yet, if men had the use of reason they pretend to, their commonwealth might be secured, at least from perishing by internal diseases."

Accompanying this change of opinion, or apparent contradiction, is a change of tone in Hobbes' language. Now we find less dispassionate analysis and more polemic—a plea for the urgent resolution of pending problems. This plea begins with the following statement in the opening paragraph of the present chapter and ends on an eloquent note of hope in the final paragraph of Part II to be quoted later.

The fault of "intestine disorder," says Hobbes, "is not in men as they are the *matter;* but as they are the *makers,* and orderers of them." In short, with proper statesmanship and the use of right principles (such as those expounded in this book), internal causes of civic dissolution might be arrested. Thus Hobbes adduces certain "causes" of dissolution, which may be construed as being directed at his sovereign.

"Among the infirmities . . . of a commonwealth," says Hobbes, "I will reckon in the first place, those that arise from an imperfect institution." What is the nature of this imperfection? Hobbes answers that it is the *want of absolute power* of the sovereign.

Hobbes then goes on to list other specific causes of dissolution. First, he cites "seditious doctrines." These include (1) the doctrine that every private man is judge of good and evil actions; (2) that whatever a man does against his conscience is sin; (3) the belief in supernatural inspiration; (4) the doctrine that the sovereign is subject to the civil laws; (5) that a private man has an absolute private property (i.e., such as to exclude the right of the sovereign over the property); and (6) the doctrine that the sovereign power may be divided.

Hobbes then adduces the imitation of neighboring nations as a cause of men's desire to alter their form of government. Hobbes is particularly anxious to guard his readers against the encroachment of the Greek and Roman ideas. "And as to rebellion in particular against monarchy," he says, "one of the most frequent causes of it is the reading of the books of policy, and histories of the ancient Greeks and Romans; from which, young men, and all others that are unprovided of the antidote of solid reason . . . receive withal a pleasing idea. . . ."

Hobbes also notes that the system of mixed government is the innovation of the Greeks and Romans. But for him, mixed government is no government at all, but "division of the commonwealth into three factions," which, to his way of thinking, spells the dissolution of it.

Another interesting source of dissolution is the popularity of powerful subjects. This is a "dangerous disease," says Hobbes, because these popular men, with flattery and reputation, seduce the people into following them and disobeying the laws. (Hobbes gives Julius Caèsar as an example.) "And this proceeding of popular, and ambitious men," says Hobbes, "is plain rebellion; and may be resembled to the effects of witchcraft." It is not surprising that Hobbes should see a greater danger in the "witchcraft" of popular government than in a monarchy. In another of his works, he defines democracy as "an aristocracy of orators."

Anticipating Rousseau, Hobbes was fearful of a pluralistic society as being unsuitable for an ideal commonwealth. (Rousseau also expounded a theory of absolute sovereignty, only his was a democratic theory, rather than monarchic.) Hobbes likens "the great number of corporations" to "many lesser commonwealths in the bowels of a greater, like worms in the entrails of a natural man."

After citing all these causes of dissolution, Hobbes tells us that in the event that the commonwealth is dissolved, whether from external or internal cause, then every man is free to protect himself "by such courses as his own discretion shall suggest unto him." This is so because "though the right of a sovereign monarch cannot be extinguished by the act of another; yet the obligation of the members may. For he that wants protection, may seek it anywhere."

COMMENT: This is perfectly consistent with his remark in Chapter XXI that "the obligation of subjects to the sovereign, is understood to last as long [as], and no longer than, the power lasteth, by which he is able to protect them." Again, at the very end of *Leviathan,* he speaks of "the mutual relation between protection and obedience; of which the condition of human nature, and the laws divine, both natural and positive, require an inviolable observation." This is, perhaps, as the philosopher Bertrand Russell notes, Hobbes' own justification of his submission to Cromwell while Charles II was in exile—"for he that wants protection, may seek it anywhere."

CHAPTER XXX. OF THE OFFICE OF THE SOVEREIGN REPRESENTATIVE

This chapter discusses in detail the duties of the sovereign. Hobbes tells us that the sovereign should provide his subjects, not only with safety, but with "other contentments of life"— and this through instruction and the laws. It is especially important that the sovereign make the people understand the reasoning behind his essential rights (i.e., that he make them understand the essence of Hobbes' political theory).

The subjects must also be taught not to try to change the government. Hobbes emphasizes that people are not necessarily safe because of the particular form of government under which they happen to live. For Hobbes, the form of government is relatively unimportant. What is important is the fact of obedience to a sovereign, whether that sovereign be democratic, aristocratic, or monarchic.

Subjects are also to be taught not to dispute the sovereign power by following one or another of their fellow subjects; to honor their parents; to avoid injuring each other; to regard as unjust overtly hostile acts and the intention to commit such acts; and finally to be charitable toward one another and "to love thy neighbor as thyself."

At this point Hobbes launches into a brief diatribe against the English universities, which taught the Scholastic philosophy to which he was opposed and against which his own work represents a revolt.

Then he goes on to say that justice must be administered equally to all the people, no matter what their degree of prestige in the commonwealth, "for in this consisteth equity, to which, as being a precept of the law of nature, a sovereign is as much a subject, as any of the meanest of his people." He also advocates public charity for those really in need of it, and urges the prevention of idleness.

> **COMMENT:**   Hobbes also suggests a remedy for the problem of population explosion. "And when all the world is overcharged with inhabitants," he says, "then the last remedy is war; which provideth for every man, by victory, or death."

Another duty of the sovereign is the making of "good laws," which he defines as "that which is needful, for the good of the people, and withal perspicuous." A "good law" is not the same as a "just law." A law is by definition just, and no law can be unjust. "The law is made by the sovereign power," says Hobbes, "and all that is done by such power is warranted, and owned by every one of the people." All this is part of the original covenant which instituted the commonwealth.

The sovereign has the right and duty to punish, but punishment should be aimed at correction, not revenge. In the event of a rebellion, Hobbes tells us, the leaders and teachers of sedition should be punished, "not the poor seduced people." He adds: "To be severe to the people is to punish that ignorance which may in great part be imputed to the sovereign whose fault it was that they were no better instructed."

The best counsel, Hobbes says, comes from the complaints of the people, "who are best acquainted with their own wants, and ought therefore, when they demand nothing in derogation of the essential rights of sovereignty, to be diligently taken notice of. For without those essential rights, as I have often before said, the commonwealth cannot at all subsist."

Finally, Hobbes declares that the relationship among different nations is like that between individual persons in the state of nature—above whom "there being no court of natural justice, but in the conscience only; where not man, but God reigneth."

CHAPTER XXXI. OF THE KINGDOM OF GOD BY NATURE

Men, says Hobbes, are subject to the divine power whether they will it or not. Those who believe in God are His subjects; those who do not are His enemies. The Word of God is declared in three ways: reason, revelation, and the voice of man who gains credibility by performing miracles.

It is important, for Hobbes, that God's right to sovereignty over the world is derived from His *power,* His omnipotence, and is justified by this fact alone. "The right of nature, whereby God reigneth over men, and punisheth those that break His laws," says Hobbes, "is to be derived, not from His creating them, as if He required obedience as of gratitude for His benefits; but from His irresistible power."

According to Hobbes, obedience to God's laws, i.e., the laws of nature, "is the greatest worship of all." We must remember at this point that, with regard to politics, what the laws of nature command men to do, essentially, is to obey the sovereign. We can see here the dovetailing of political and religious obligation in Hobbes' theory.

"Seeing a commonwealth is but one person," Hobbes says, "it ought also to exhibit to God but one worship." This should be a public worship, and uniform, laid down by the sovereign, who is also the sovereign interpreter of the word of God on earth.

COMMENT: Like Plato, Cicero, and Machiavelli, Hobbes wrote his great political treatise with the hope that some day a ruler would read and follow it in practice. He assures us that the book is sufficiently short and clear so as not to be difficult to read.

Then he tells us why his book is more worthy than any written by the Greeks and Romans. *Leviathan,* he says, is the first attempt that has ever been made to "put into order, and sufficiently or probably proved all the theorems of moral doctrine, that men may learn thereby, both how to govern, and how to obey." And he ends Part II with the following wish: "I . . . hope, that one time or other this writing of mine may fall into the hands of a sovereign who will consider it himself (for it is short, and I think clear) without the help of any interested or envious interpreter; and by the exercise of entire sovereignty, in protecting the public teaching of it, convert this truth of speculation into the utility of practice."

The last two books of *Leviathan* deal with what one might call "political theology." In Part III, "Of a Christian Commonwealth," Hobbes expounds the theory of the supremacy of the state over the church, and demolishes the time-honored notions of a universal church, papal supremacy over the king, and papal infallibility. In Part IV, "Of the Kingdom of Darkness," Hobbes concentrates his attack upon the Church of Rome and its philosophical patron, Aristotle, to whom Hobbes usually refers as the author of "vain philosophy."

ESSAY QUESTIONS AND ANSWERS

1. In Hobbes' system, how does reason deliver man out of the state of nature and guide him toward a life of peace and security?

ANSWER: Man's exercise of reason is the turning point in his struggle for peace and security. But reason does not determine his fate. It merely directs him to goals already determined by the passions. Thus, to understand the precise role reason plays in the state of nature prior to man's entrance into civil society, one must inquire into its relation to the passions.

Hobbes tells us that man has three "principal causes of quarrel" in the state of nature. These are *competition* (for gain), *diffidence* (for safety), and *glory* (for reputation). It is these passions, we are told, that incline men to war. Men also possess other passions that incline them toward peace: *fear* (of death), *desire* (of things leading to a more commodious life), and *hope* (of obtaining them by hard work).

The role of reason is not to "govern" or "control" these passions, for it cannot, but rather to discover the means of best gratifying them. The question is which passions to gratify: the war-inclining passions or the peace-inclining passions? According to Hobbes, the peace-inclining passions will ultimately prevail over the war-inclining passions, as a consequence of man's aversion to war gained from his bitter experience in the state of nature. Reason then steps in to serve its master passions, i.e., the peace-inclining passions. It "suggests" the "convenient articles of peace upon which men may be drawn to agreement." These articles are otherwise called "laws of nature," and are none other, says Hobbes, than "precepts of reason."

Inasmuch as these laws of nature provide the basis for social contract and thus open the way for a civil society, reason is the key to man's political salvation. But the redeeming function of reason is entirely contingent upon the triumph of the right kind of passions. Reason, for Hobbes, can but serve and guide the passions; it cannot conquer them, as was alleged in traditional moral philosophy.

2. Discuss Hobbes' conception of "commonwealth by acquisition" in light of his theory of social contract.

ANSWER: For Hobbes, the only way a government may come into being is through the voluntary agreement of men who are to be subjected to it. It is out of their own calculation of self-interest that men are induced to join together to form a commonwealth. When men create society out of the anarchy of the state of nature, by each one making a covenant with everyone else, this is called a "commonwealth by institution." It is clear that I am morally bound to obey the sovereign of that commonwealth, for I am the author of that power; disobedience would be tantamount to self-contradiction.

But there is another kind of commonwealth, "commonwealth by acquisition." What distinguishes this commonwealth from the other is simply that it is created by force. That being so, does the conqueror have a moral authority over me? Do I owe him obedience? Later, Locke and Rousseau thought not, but for Hobbes the answer is Yes. This is so, says Hobbes, because each man who has been subjugated by the conqueror had the freedom to choose between two alternatives: risking death for the sake of honor by resisting the conqueror, or securing his life by gracefully surrendering himself to the conqueror. When one is subjugated by force, it implies that he has chosen the latter course. This was a free choice, and it amounts to a "covenant" with the conqueror, for he has gained his life and protection at the price of obedience.

Consequently, a commonwealth by acquisition is as legitimate as a commonwealth by institution. The only difference between the two is this: When one enters a commonwealth by institution his motive is fear of all others; when he enters a commonwealth by acquisition his motive is fear of only one person, the conqueror. In both cases, it is one's *fear of death* and *desire of self-preservation* that impel him to make the covenant. In both cases, the moving force is self-interest. In both cases, what gives the government its legitimacy, i.e., a moral authority to exercise its power of coercion over its subjects, is *covenant*.

Is there such a thing as an illegitimate government? Hobbes would answer that the only illegitimate government (one that has no moral authority over its subjects) is that which is incapable of protecting its people. The people exchange obedience for protection, which is their sole reason for leaving the state of nature and surrendering their natural rights to use all means necessary to protect themselves. When a government has proved itself to be incompetent as a preserver of peace and order, it has proved itself to be no government in the proper sense of the word. When this happens, the people would be wise to go out and choose a real sovereign elsewhere. The Bible says, "The powers that be are ordained of God" (*Epist. to Romans*, Chap. XIII, 1). Hobbes seems to be saying, "The powers that be are legitimate." Thus, in Hobbes, liberty and necessity, consent and force, power and legitimacy go hand in hand, without being mutually exclusive.

SELECTED BIBLIOGRAPHY
THE PRINCIPAL WORKS OF HOBBES

1640, *The Elements of Law,* first published in England in 1650 as two treatises: *On Human Nature* and *De Corpore Politica.*

1642, *De Cive* (in Latin; English edition published in 1651). Paperback.

1646, *Of Liberty and Necessity.*

1651, *Leviathan.* Paperback.

1655, *De Corpore* (in Latin).

1658, *De Homine* (in Latin).

1660, *Behemoth, or The Long Parliament.*

1666, *A Dialogue Between a Philosopher and a Student of Common Laws of England,* published posthumously in 1681.

SELECTED RECENT WORKS ON HOBBES

Laird, John, *Hobbes* (London, 1934).

Peters, Richard, *Hobbes* (London, 1956).

Plamenatz, John, *Man and Society* (New York, 1963), Vol. I, chap. 4.

Sabine, George H., *A History of Political Theory,* 3rd ed. (New York, 1961), chap. 23.

Stephen, Sir Leslie, *Hobbes* (London, 1904).

Strauss, Leo, *The Political Philosophy of Hobbes,* trans. Elsa Sinclair (Oxford, 1936).

Strauss, Leo, and Cropsey, Joseph (eds.), *History of Political Philosophy* (Chicago, 1963), pp. 354-378.

Warrender, Howard, *The Political Philosophy of Hobbes: His Theory of Obligation* (Oxford, 1957).

JOHN LOCKE: INTRODUCTORY

LIFE AND TIMES

BACKGROUND: The seventeenth century was a century of dramatic change in England. In 1642 a bloody civil war broke out between the forces of the king and parliament. The king, Charles I, lost, and in 1649 paid for his failure with his head. There followed the Puritan dictatorship of Cromwell and the restoration of the Stuarts in 1660. The Stuarts reigned until 1688, the year of the so-called Glorious Revolution, which saw the deposition of James II.

The crown worn by the new monarchs, William and Mary, did not symbolize the same power that it had for their predecessors. To gain the throne they were forced to sign the famous Bill of Rights and accept the supremacy of Parliament. Absolute monarchy was dead. So was the theory of the divine right of kings. A new ideology of secular government with limited powers was in vogue. And a new middle class had risen to take its place at the seat of power. The philosopher most commonly associated with both is John Locke.

EARLY LIFE: Locke was born in 1632 at Wrington of a middle-class yeoman family. He attended grammar school at nearby Bristol, and later took his preparatory education at the Westminster School in London. Locke was seventeen when Charles was executed. In 1652, at the age of twenty, Locke took a scholarship at Christ Church College, Oxford, where he was given a classical and Scholastic education. He did well enough in his studies to be retained upon graduation as a tutor at Christ Church. Soon he became a lecturer in Greek and Latin. His association with the university lasted until 1684.

Locke was a man of many interests. At Oxford, he was first drawn to the study of theology, then to medicine (he became an assistant to an Oxford physician). He also showed a proficiency in science (physics and chemistry), and had some interest in political problems. In 1665, he received an appointment as Secretary to the British ambassador at the Court of Brandenburg.

SHAFTESBURY: Locke was successful at Brandenburg, but his appointment lapsed the following year and he returned to Oxford. It was at this time that he met Lord Ashley, later the first Earl of Shaftesbury. Both Locke and Shaftesbury were men of penetrating intellect, and they struck up a deep and lasting friendship. Locke's close association with Shaftesbury was to change his life completely.

Shaftesbury (or Ashley as he was then known) suffered from a liver ailment which might have been fatal. But after Locke had gained his confidence, he persuaded Shaftesbury to undergo an operation, which miraculously saved his life. Shaftesbury was a leading political figure of his day, and, next to the king, probably the most powerful man in England. He had been a high official under Cromwell, but then helped to bring about the Restoration. He saw that Locke's best talents were being wasted in medicine, and that his broad and insightful views on man and society suited him to a political career.

From then on, Locke's fortunes were inextricably tied to those of Shaftesbury. He was soon offered the post of tutor for Shaftesbury's son, and took up residence in London under retainer from Shaftesbury. There he composed an *Essay on Toleration* and other works in conjunction with his benefactor. At this time, too, Shaftesbury brought about Locke's appointment as a Fellow of the Royal Society.

POLITICAL ACTIVITIES: In 1672, Shraftesbury became Lord Chancellor and held the job for three years. Locke was named Secretary to the Board of Trade. At the end of the three years, there came a decline in Shaftesbury's prestige, and so Locke was also out of a job.

Locke took this occasion to go to Europe. He suffered from asthma, and the trip—ostensibly at least—was taken for reasons of health. He stayed on the Continent four years, during which time he worked on his masterpiece, the *Essay Concerning Human Understanding*. He spent two of those years at Montpellier in southern France and one in Paris.

In 1679, Shaftesbury returned to power, and Locke returned to England. But neither was to be there long. A bitter dispute had broken out over the succession to the throne. Many influential men urged the king to name his illegitimate half-brother, Monmouth, as the heir apparent. Charles refused, maintained loyalty to his brother James, a Catholic, and sought to increase his control over the machinery of government at the expense of Parliament.

Shaftesbury was a leader of the Monmouth party. He was banished by the king, and had to take refuge in Holland, where he soon died. It is doubtful that Locke played much of a part in the Monmouth conspiracy. But his close association to Shaftesbury made him suspect, and so he, too, found it wise to seek refuge in Holland. There, Locke was a hunted man. The king, while stripping Locke of his Oxford position, sought to have him extradited for allegedly plotting against the throne. So Locke took to hiding, and for a time lived under an assumed name. All the while he was composing his *Essay on Human Understanding* and other works. His first of four *Letters Concerning Toleration* was published in Latin, and so was an abstract of the *Essay*. Locke returned from exile shortly after the revolution of 1688. After turning down a diplomatic post, he was made Commissioner of Appeals.

YEARS OF FRUITION: Within the next four years, Locke completed all his most important works. In 1689, an English version of the first *Letter Concerning Toleration* was published. A year later came the *Two Treatises of Government* and the *Essay*. In 1693, there appeared a less famous work called *Thoughts on Education*.

OLD AGE: Locke's health was now beginning to fail him. In

1691, he moved into the country, at Oates Manor in Essex, and, although still in public service, spent less and less of his time dealing with the affairs of state. He continued to work at the *Essay*. A second edition was printed in 1694, and two more appeared within his lifetime. His views, especially those with religious implications, engendered considerable controversy. His second and third *Letters Concerning Toleration* were products of an exchange between him and Bishop Stillingfleet of Worcester over the religious issue. He also addressed a series of letters to Isaac Newton.

Locke reluctantly came out of semiretirement in 1696 to accept a post as Commissioner on Trade and Plantations. It took up most of his healthy hours, and these were becoming increasingly few. Finally, in 1700, he resigned, and spent the rest of his days in retirement at Oates. He died in 1704, and was buried near Oates next to the parish church of High Laver.

PHILOSOPHY

THEORY OF KNOWLEDGE: So influential has Locke been as a political philosopher and ideologist that it tends to overshadow his enormous contribution to the theory of knowledge, where, indeed, his true greatness lies.

Locke is considered to be the first great empiricist. He took upon himself the task of vindicating the achievements of modern science—gained by men like Harvey, Boyle, and Newton—by teaching that all knowledge comes from sense experience. Locke rejected the prevailing Cartesian theory of innate knowledge, and in Book I of his *Essay Concerning Human Understanding* he shows how worthless it was as an explanation of the source of our knowledge.

In Book II of the *Essay*, Locke argues that all knowledge can be traced back to only one source, sense perception. Knowledge of the world about us, he says, begins in sense perception. It does not begin in innate knowledge of maxims or general principles; nor does it proceed from syllogistic reasoning from such principles. The mind at birth, Locke argues, is a *tabula rasa,* or blank tablet.

But not only do we perceive the world about us; we also perceive the operation of our own minds. This is a kind of perception known as introspection, or, as Locke calls it, "reflection." Abstract ideas, such as infinity, power, and cause and effect, are products of reflection. Although these may appear to be beyond sense experience in their origin, Locke argues that they must have been born in sense experience. They are brought about through memory and its attendant activities, such as contemplation, distinction, and comparison.

EMPIRICISM AND RATIONALISM: However, Locke's political theory is not based on his epistemological premise. His political theory is rationalistic, that is to say, based on a theory of natural law which is discovered by reason. But as we have just seen, Locke was an empiricist in his theory of knowledge, i.e., he believed that the source of all knowledge is ultimately sense experience. This lack of consistency, however, did not seem to bother Locke.

Hobbes' greatness as a political thinker lay in the skillful manner in which he deduced his political arguments from first principles, *viz.,* body and motion. This method he likened to geometry. However, Locke made no such attempt at being systematic. Moreover, Locke possessed neither the clarity and logic of Hobbes nor the literary brilliance of Rousseau. But he possessed a quality neither of them had—common sense. Through the use of common sense, Locke was able to discern principles of the middle-class political revolution of this time and drive them home in terms of the prevailing political idioms. In short, Locke was a clever ideologist.

HOOKER AND HOBBES: Locke never failed to acknowledge his indebtedness to the "judicious" Richard Hooker (1553-1600), the Elizabethan theologian, who was his greatest source of inspiration. It was through Hooker that Locke became acquainted with the medieval conception of natural law. It was also through Hooker that Locke learned the all-important distinction between government and society, and the idea that government must be held accountable to society as its trustor. Without Hooker's ideas, it would have been nearly impossible for Locke to refute Hobbes' theory of absolute sovereignty.

Of his indebtedness to Hobbes himself, Locke was far more grudging in his acknowledgment. In spite of his vehement objections to Hobbes' theory of absolute sovereignty and the psychological premises underlying this doctrine, Locke's political philosophy must be understood as a continuation of the Hobbesian tradition.

Apart from the fact that Locke employed Hobbes' concepts of state of nature, social contract, and natural right, Locke was in complete agreement with Hobbes on two basic assumptions. First, both Locke and Hobbes believed that political society is not a natural event, but a human invention, or artifact—even though, as Locke admitted, once made, society may "act according to its own nature."

Secondly, Locke, like Hobbes, used the individual, and not any group, as the basic political unit, and defined the goals of society solely in terms of individual interest. He accepted Hobbes' doctrine of self-preservation as the primary human urge and sanctified this passion as the primary object of social policy—without having taken the trouble, as Hobbes had done, to deduce this principle through the painful process of reasoning.

LIMITED GOVERNMENT: But that is about as far as Locke would travel with Hobbes. Hobbes, as we have seen, used his theory of contract only to propose a frightening doctrine of absolute sovereignty. But Locke argued that absolute government is far worse than the original state of nature, with all its inconveniences. He argued that government is not only created by the people, but it must remain perpetually accountable to them.

In short, government must be not absolute, but conditional and limited in its power and authority.

Locke was able to put forward this argument because he asserted that the original state of nature was not so hopelessly anarchic as Hobbes had maintained. On the contrary, Locke thought the state of nature to be characterized by "peace, good will, mutual assistance, and preservation." Under Locke's law of nature, all men were equal and possessed an equal right to life, liberty, and property. But men did not always agree on the meaning of natural law, and in the absence of a common judge, each man was free to interpret and execute the law of nature in his own selfish way. Understandably, this led to a condition of anarchy. So men formed civil society and gave up their right to exercise the law of nature individually in return for the preservation by the community of their lives, liberties, and estates. The community, or civil society, thus created acts through its majority, and its primary and immediate function is to create a government as its trustee. Once the government is created by the community, the "supreme power" (Locke never uses the term "sovereignty" as did Hobbes) resides in that government as long as it functions as a government, i.e., as long as it protects the property of individual members of society. Behind the government stands the community, possessed with the latent "supreme power" of dissolving the government if it should act contrary to its trust. Such dissolving of government, or revolution, is justified only when the government endeavors to invade the property of the members of the community and to make itself the "arbitrary disposer of the lives, liberties, and fortunes of the people."

PLACE IN HISTORY

GENERAL IMPACT: There are not many philosophers in the history of Western philosophy who had as great an impact on the minds and institutions of future generations as John Locke. In his own time, Locke's chief philosophical objective was to refute the rationalistic epistemology of the Cartesians on the one hand,

and the theory of political absolutism of Hobbes on the other. His work in both these areas proved to be immensely successful in his own lifetime, but the greatest impact of his work was felt after the seventeenth century.

EPISTEMOLOGY: His empiricism became the groundwork for the skepticism of Berkeley and Hume, and also left a great impression upon the French *philosophes* and the English Philosophical Radicals. Indirectly, through the work of Hume, Locke also exerted a tremendous influence on Kant, whose "critical philosophy" is meant to be a synthesis of the opposing philosophical traditions embodied in the rationalism of Descartes and Leibnitz and the empiricism of Locke, Berkeley, and Hume.

POLITICS: Locke's influence as a political thinker was even more far-reaching. The internal structure of his doctrines was pretty thoroughly demolished by the supreme skeptic, Hume. It was commonplace in England during the latter part of the eighthteenth century and in the nineteenth century to ridicule the whole concept of social contract. Bentham, for instance, declared that Locke's idea of natural right was nothing but "rhetorical nonsense upon stilts." But the practical value of Locke's political doctrines more than offset the weakness of their logical and scientific foundations.

Not only were the Lockean doctrines of natural right, natural law, and right of rebellion to be incorporated in the constitutions of many American colonies, but they even found their way into the American Declaration of Independence. Even Locke's terminology is evident in these documents of American history.

PROPERTY: Lockes' theory of property had a twofold effect. On the one hand, it advanced the cause of capitalism by its defense of the sanctity of private property and the inviolability of property from government intrusion. On the other hand, ironically enough, his labor theory of value was used by Marx and others in their arguments for communism. If a thing gains its worth solely as a consequence of labor expended in producing it, does it not follow, asked Marx, that the worker, and not the capitalist, is entitled to the full return from the product of his labor?

LOCKE AS A SYMBOL: Above and beyond these specific areas of influence, Locke's name continues to symbolize the ideals of tolerance, individualism, right of dissent, majority rule and others which are integral parts of the liberal political tradition of Western society.

TREATISE OF CIVIL GOVERNMENT

BOOK I

COMMENT: Book I of the *Two Treatises* is usually referred to as the *First Treatise,* or *Of Government.* Like Books III and IV of Hobbes' *Leviathan,* however, this book is seldom read. It is devoted primarily to a refutation of the arguments of Sir Robert Filmer as presented in his *Patriarcha, or The Natural Power of Kings,* that kings rule by divine right inherited from Adam.

According to Filmer, God originally bestowed the kingly power upon Adam, from whom it descended to his heir, and ultimately reached the various monarchs of modern times. Consequently, for Filmer, the sole source of regal authority is subjection of children to parents.

Book II of the *Two Treatises,* usually called the *Second Treatise,* or *Of Civil Government,* is Locke's main political work. In this book, Locke refutes the absolute theory of government, particularly that found in *Hobbes' Leviathan,* even though the latter work is not mentioned. The book begins with a brief summary of the argument of the *First Treatise.*

CHAPTER I.   OF POLITICAL POWER

Locke makes four points in refutation of Filmer's divine right theory. First, he argues that Adam did not have such domain over the world or his children as is pretended, either by the right of fatherhood or by the gift of God. Secondly, even if he had such domain, his heirs had no right to it. Thirdly, even if the heirs did have right to such domain, there is no natural or positive law that determines the right of succession. And, finally, even if the right of succession could be determined, the eldest line of Adam's posterity could not be. Consequently, political power is different from the power of the father over his children, of the husband over his wife, of the master over his servant, or of the lord over his slave.

Having thus demolished Filmer's divine-right doctrine, Locke must now explain what he considers to be the legitimate foundation of government. He begins this task with a definition of political power: "Political power, then, I take to be a right of making laws with penalties of death, and consequently all less penalties, for the regulating and preserving of property, and of employing the force of the community in the execution of such laws, and in the defense of the commonwealth from foreign injury, and all this only for the public good."

With this definition of political power, Locke sets the stage for the *Second Treatise*. This is the theme; what follows is elaboration on the theme. Like Hobbes, Locke begins his discourse with an inquiry into the meaning of the "state of nature."

CHAPTER II. OF THE STATE OF NATURE

The natural condition of men is depicted as "a state of perfect freedom to order their actions and dispose of their possessions and persons as they think fit, within the bounds of the law of nature, without asking leave, or depending upon the will of any other man."

It is also a state of equality, "wherein all the power and jurisdiction is reciprocal, no one having more than another." In that state there is neither subordination nor subjection, for being creatures of the same species, men are "born to all the same advantages of nature and the use of the same faculties."

Locke hastens to add that a state of liberty is not the same as a state of license. "Though man in that state have an uncontrollable liberty to dispose of his person or possession," says Locke, "Yet, he has not liberty to destroy himself, or so much as any creature in his possession, but where some nobler use than its bare preservation calls for." What is the source of this moral inhibition? Locke answers that "the state of nature has a law of nature to govern it, which obliges every one; and reason, which is that law, teaches all mankind who will but consult it, that, being all equal and independent, no one ought to harm another in his life, health, liberty, or posessions." Every man is bound by this law *to preserve himself,* and, "when his own preservation comes not in competition . . . to preserve the rest of mankind, and not, unless it be to do justice on an offender, take away or impair the life, or what tends to the preservation of the life, the liberty, health, limb, or goods of another."

> **COMMENT:** In defending man's basic right of self-preservation, Locke is following Hobbes with no modification. Even when he speaks of man's duty to preserve the rest of mankind, he states the priority of self-preservation in most unmistakable terms: "to preserve the rest of mankind" is allowed "when his own preservation comes not in competition."
>
> And in Chapter IX of the *First Treatise,* he goes to the extent of saying, "The first and strongest desire God planted in men, and wrought into the very principles of their nature," is "that of self-preservation."

In this state of nature, however, "the execution of the law of nature is . . . put into every man's hand, whereby every one has a right to punish the transgressions of that law to such a degree as may hinder its violation." This follows from Locke's definition of the state of nature as a state where "men live together according to reason, without a common superior on earth with authority to judge between them" (Chapter III).

Suppose someone in the state of nature has transgressed the law of nature and "declares himself to live by another rule than that of common reason and equity, which is that measure God has set to the actions of men?" In such a case, "every man hath a right to punish the offender, and be executioner of the law of nature." To this strange doctrine—*viz.,* that in the state of

nature every one has the executive power of the law of nature,"
—says Locke, "I doubt not but it will be objected that it is unreasonable for men to be judges in their own cases, that self-love
will make men partial to themselves and their friends." It is to
remedy these great "inconveniences of the state of nature" that
civil society is instituted.

And an absolute monarchy, by its very nature, is not such a
remedy, but itself an inconvenience: "Absolute monarchies are
but men, and if government is to be the remedy of those evils
which necessarily follow from men's being judges of their own
cases, and the state of nature is therefore not to be endured, I
desire to know what kind of government that is, and how much
better it is than the state of nature, where one man commanding
a multitude, has the liberty to be judge in his own case, and
may do to all his subjects whatever he pleases, without the least
questions or control of those who execute his pleasure; and in
whatever he doth, whether led by reason, mistake, or passion,
must be submitted to, which men in the state of nature are not
bound to do one to another?"

> **COMMENT:**   It is clear, then, that, for Locke, as it was
> for Hobbes, the state of nature was never meant to be a
> historical description of the life of primitive people.
> Rather, it is a concept which has a logical value as a work-
> ing hypothesis. Specifically, for Locke, it means the ab-
> sence of a civil society: "All men are naturally in that
> state, and remain so, till, by their own consents they make
> themselves members of some politic society." Agreeing
> with Hobbes, Locke describes the relationships among
> the rulers of independent governments as one of the state
> of nature and says that "the world never was, nor ever will
> be, without numbers of men in that state."

CHAPTER III.   OF THE STATE OF WAR

The state of war is not a pretty state. It is, Locke tells us, a state
of enmity and destruction, where one declares by word or action
"a sedate, settled design upon another man's life." Once this

design is manifest, that person exposes his life to the other person's executive power to punish. By his efforts to subdue the other, to make him his slave, and to take away his freedom, he puts himself in a state of war with the other.

Obviously, the state of war and the state of nature are not the same. Locke complains that some have confused the two: "And here we have the plain difference between the state of nature and the state of war, which however some men have confounded, are as far distant as a state of peace, good-will, mutual assistance and preservation, and a state of enmity, malice, violence and mutual destruction, are one from another." The state of nature is simply one in which men live together according to reason "without a common superior on earth with authority to judge between them." The state of war, however, denotes the existence of *force,* "or declared design of force, upon the person of another, where there is no common superior on earth to appeal to for relief. . . . It is the want of such an appeal [that] gives a man the right of war even against an aggressor, though he be in society and a fellow-subject." Further on, Locke clarifies his meaning: "Want of a common judge with authority puts all men in a state of nature; force without right, upon a man's person, makes a state of war, both where is, and is not, a common judge."

> **COMMENT:**   In other words, the opposite of the state of nature is civil society. This is made explicit in Chapter VII, where Locke says, "Those who are united into one body, and have a common established law and judicature to appeal to, with authority to decide controversies between them and punish offenders, are in civil society one with another; but those who have no such common appeal —I mean on earth—are still in the state of nature. . . ."

Now the state of war is something else, for it is not defined in terms of the existence of a common judge. The distinguishing criterion of the state of war is *the use of force without right or justice.* Thus in Chapter XIII we hear Locke remark that "the use of force without authority always puts him that uses it into a state of war, as the aggressor, and renders him liable to be treated accordingly." Again, in Chapter XVI, he says, "It is the unjust use of force, then, that puts a man into the state of war with another. . . ." And in Chapter XIX: "Whosoever uses force without right, as everyone does in society who does it without law, puts himself into a state of war with those against whom he so uses it. . . ."

From the above definitions we can see that both in the state of nature and in civil society a state of peace and a state of war may prevail *at different times*. So much is clear. However, Locke is partly to blame for the alleged confusion, for it is he who paints the state of nature in two different ways: in some places it is described as a place where men live in a condition of "peace, good will, mutual assistance and preservation," whereas in other places—where he seeks to demonstrate the "inconveniences" of living without a common superior—he depicts it as a state of war in the manner of Hobbes.

CHAPTER IV. OF SLAVERY

The title of this chapter is misleading. It really concerns freedom, rather than slavery. A man is naturally free when he has only the law of nature for his rule. This makes him free from any superior power on earth and from the will of all other men. The liberty of man in society is for him to be under no other legislative power but that established by his own consent in the commonwealth. This means being not under the domination of any will, or under the restraint of any law, but that enacted by the legislative power according to the trust put in it.

Freedom from arbitrary power, says Locke, is so necessary to man's preservation that he cannot live without it.

Locke does get around to talking about slavery toward the end of the chapter. He says no man can enslave himself by his own consent because he does not have such power over his own life. Finally, Locke defines the perfect condition of slavery as the state of war continued between lawful conqueror and captive.

CHAPTER V.   OF PROPERTY

If God gave reason and revelation to men in common, Locke asks, how does it come about that they have property? Having said that the earth belongs to everyone in common, Locke must now "show how men might come to have a property in several parts of that which God gave to mankind in common, and that without any express compact of all the commoners."

The earth is common to all men, says Locke, "yet every man has a property in his own person; this nobody has any right to but himself." Now, the *labor* of one's body is unquestionably his own. Consequently, "whatever . . . he removes out of the state that nature hath provided and left it in," so he tells us, "he hath mixed his labor with, and joined to it something that is his own, and thereby makes it his property." In other words, property is the product of the union of what is private (labor) and what is common (the land)—"at least where there is enough, and as good left in common for others."

Does one have a right to acquire as much as he wants? The answer is No: "As much as any one can make use of to any advantage of life before it spoils, so much he may by his labor fix a property in: whatever is beyond this, is more than his share, and belongs to others. Nothing was made by God for man to spoil or destroy."

This principle applies both to the accumulation of certain goods out of the common land and to the appropriation of land itself. "Before the appropriation of land," says Locke, "he who gathered as much of the wild fruit, killed, caught, or tamed as many of the beasts as he could . . . by placing any of his labor on them, did thereby acquire a property in them." But, he continues, "If they perished in his possession without their due use . . . he offended against the common law of nature, and was liable to be punished." Likewise, as for the possession of land, "whatsoever he enclosed and could feed and make use of, the cattle and product was also his. But if either the grass of his enclosure rotted on the ground, or the fruit of his planting perished without gathering and laying up, this part of the earth, notwithstanding his enclosure, was still to be looked on as waste, and might be the possession of any other."

Labor, for Locke, does not merely draw a line between what is private and what is public: it creates value, makes worth out of something which is otherwise completely worthless. Land without labor puts into it, says Locke, is "scarcely worth anything." "Nature and the earth furnished only the almost worthless materials as in themselves." It is labor "that puts the difference of value on everything."

> COMMENT: This idea, that the value of a product depends upon the labor expended on it, is known as the "labor theory of value," often associated with Marx and Ricardo. Locke was not, however, the originator of this theory: its rudiments can be traced back as far as St. Thomas. It was one form of labor theory of value that led the medieval Schoolmen to condemn moneylending and speculating as immoral. Later, Ricardo and Marx articulated the labor theory of value to oppose landowners and capitalists, respectively.

Locke next discusses the origin of the use of money—"some lasting thing that men might keep without spoiling, and that, by mutual consent, men would take in exchange for the truly useful but perishable supports of life." Locke is by no means unaware of the sociopolitical consequences of the use of money: inequality. "And as different degrees of industry were apt to give men possesions in different proportions," says Locke, "so this invention of money gave them the opportunity to continue and enlarge them." In fact, the author of the labor theory of value now appears to justify the inequality of wealth on moral grounds: "It is plain that the consent of men have agreed to a disproportionate and unequal possession of the earth. . . ."

CHAPTER VI.   OF PATERNAL POWER

Locke is concerned in this chapter to trace the derivation of paternal power—or, as he points out, what should more correctly be called "parental" power, because mother and father are equally responsible for the welfare of the offspring.

The problem arises from Locke's assertion in the second chapter that all men are by nature equal. If this be so, how can anyone have power over another? How, for instance, can the parent have power over the children? Locke replies by qualifying his assertion concerning the equality of men: "Though I have said above (Chapter II) that all men by nature are equal, I cannot be supposed to understand all sorts of equality." He goes on to point out that age or virtue may give some men a "just precedency" over others. For example, children are not equal to their parents: "Children, I confess, are not born in this full state of equality, though they are born to it. Their parents have a sort of rule and jurisdiction over them when they come into the world, and for some time after, but 'tis but a temporary one." In other words, they grow into equality; age and reason bring them to it.

In his search for a proper conception of the role and scope of paternal power, Locke now takes us to a brief discussion of the meaning of law. His definition of law is at direct odds with the purely negative definition of law as put forward by Hobbes. "For law, in its true notion," says Locke, "is not so much the limitation as the direction of a free and intelligent agent to his proper interest, and prescribes no farther than is for the general good of those under that law." Locke goes on to observe that "could they be happier without it, the law as an useless thing would of itself vanish; and that ill deserves the name of confinement which hedges us in only from bogs and precipices."

In sum, the end of law is "not to abolish or restrain, but to preserve and enlarge freedom."

Now, if the end of law, and indeed, the end of any political community, is the preservation and enlargement of freedom, by what right do parents have power over their offspring? Locke replies that the power of parents over their children "arises from that duty which is incumbent on them, to take care of their offspring during the imperfect state of childhood." All parents are under an obligation, "by the law of nature," to preserve, nourish, and educate their children, till the defects of their youth are removed by their growth and age. Maturity means the attainment of a "state of reason," or an "age of discretion" (the age of twenty-one, as a general rule). When one has reached that stage, he is expected to have the capacity to know his rights and obligations under the law of his society. And now the father and son are considered to be "equally free." "Till then," however, "we see the law allows the son to have no will, but he is to be guided by the will of his father or guardian, who is to understand for him."

> COMMENT: The significance of this chapter lies in its rejection of the idea—which was Filmer's—that sons can never be free of paternal power even after they have reached adulthood. For Filmer the rights of a king are the same as those of a father; he then went on to defend the theory of divine right of kings in terms of paternal power.

CHAPTER VII. OF POLITICAL OR CIVIL SOCIETY

In this chapter Locke lists the different types of society—(1) between man and wife, (2) between parents and children, (3) between master and servant, and (4) political society. This last, political society, is fundamentally different from the rest. We will take these in order as they are presented in this chapter. But we must first consider, as Locke does, why men enter into society at all. His answer is that the inclination to enter into society is part of human nature as determined by his Creator.

For "God having made man such a creature, that in His own judgment it was not good for him to be alone, put him under strong obligations of necessity, convenience, and inclination to drive him into society, as well as fitted him with understanding and language to continue and enjoy it."

The first type of society is that between man and wife. Locke calls it the conjugal society. He defines it as a voluntary compact between man and woman. Other animals are not dependent on a continued relationship; only man is. This is the case, we are told, because new children are being conceived before previous ones are out of their dependency. Locke finds this characteristic only of man.

The second type of society, that between parents and children, has been treated in Chapter VI. Here Locke only refers the reader to that chapter. The third type of society is that between master and servant. There are two separate master-slave relationships, one involving a free man and the other involving a genuine slave. A free man makes himself a servant to another by selling to him, for a certain period of time, a service which he undertakes to do in exchange for wages to be paid by the master. This gives the master only temporary power, and a power no greater than that stipulated in the contract. The second master-slave relationship is that involving a real slave. The slave, according to Locke, is under the absolute dominion of the master, and is not a part of civil society.

Political society is different in kind from the other three. Locke makes obvious the relevance of man's prepolitical condition to the political society by declaring that the primary aim of men in entering into society is the preservation of their property. Here, as elsewhere, Locke uses the word *property* broadly to include "life, liberty, and estate." In fact, the preservation of the property is the very essence of a political society, for "no political society can be, nor subsist, without having in itself the power to preserve the property."

The institution of a political society involves the preemption of the private judgment of every particular member. "There, and there only, is political society," asys Locke, "where every one of the members hath quitted this natural power, resigned it up into the hands of the community in all cases that exclude him not from appealing for protection to the law established by it; and thus all private judgment of every particular member being excluded, the community comes to be umpire."

Specifically, the civil, or political, society possesses the power to "set down what punishment shall belong to the several transgressions . . . (which is the power of making laws)," and the power to execute these punishments. Herein lies the foundation of the *legislative* and *executive* powers of civil society.

> COMMENT: Locke could not abandon the subject of the origin of civil society without taking a parting shot at the theorists of absolute monarchy. He declares that absolute monarchy is inconsistent with civil society and, consequently, "no form of civil government at all." His argument is that the purpose of civil society is to set up a known authority to which every one may appeal. But an absolute prince has no one to appeal to: "For he being supposed to have all, both legislative and executive power in himself alone, there is no judge to be found. . . ." "Such a man," says Locke, "however entitled—Czar, or Grand Seignior, or how you please—is as much in the state of nature, with all under his dominion, as he is with the rest of mankind."

CHAPTER VIII.   OF THE BEGINNING OF POLITICAL SOCIETIES

> COMMENT: This chapter contains two important doctrines closely associated with the name of the author. One is the doctrine of *government by consent* and the other the doctrine of *majority rule.* An examination of these two concepts will also help us understand Locke's theory of

social contract—which has been subject to many faulty interpretations in the hands of uncritical commentators—for they are the key to the latter concept.

First, Locke explains how men leave the state of nature and enter into a *community:* "Men being . . . by nature all free, equal, and independent, no one can be out of this estate, and subjected to the political power of another, without his own consent." Rather, says Locke, men "agree" with other men "to join and unite into a community for their comfortable, safe, and peaceable living one amongst another, in a secure enjoyment of their properties, and a greater security against any that are not of it."

> **COMMENT:** By "agreement" Locke means nothing less than a unanimous agreement, of every man with every other man. What about those who refuse to join in this endeavor? Locke's answer is simple and is identical with that of Hobbes: "The rest . . . are left as they were in the liberty of the state of nature," and consequently, there is no unfairness done to them by those who have together contracted into the community.

What is the nature of this community? Does it bind the actions of its members? Obviously, it does and it must, for otherwise what is the good of creating it? Then what is the nature of political obligation in it? Locke's answer lies in his doctrine of *majority rule.* "And thus every man," says Locke, "by consenting with others to make one body politic under one government, puts himself under an obligation to every one of that society, to submit to the determination of the majority, and to be concluded by it." The majority rule must prevail, "for where the majority cannot conclude the rest, there they cannot act as one body, and consequently will be immediately dissolved."

> **COMMENT:** If the reader will turn to Chapter XVIII of *Leviathan,* he will see that both these ideas—namely, those relating to how the community (or "congregation"

for Hobbes) comes into being and how it binds the actions of its members—were already set forth by Hobbes.

The next question is: what is the end of this community, or "politic society"? Whereas Locke himself does not elaborate on the precise nature of a community in and of itself, there is no question as to its function, and that is *to create a government*. In Chapter VII, for instance, he speaks of men entering into society "to make one people, one body politic, under one supreme government, or else when any one joins himself to, and incorporates with, any government already made." And again, in the present chapter, he says that only such a society "could give beginning to any lawful government in the world."

COMMENT: When Locke says "or else when any one joins himself to, and incorporates with, any government already made," he is referring to the traditional, i.e., medieval, contract theory, sometimes known as "governmental contract," in contradistinction to the modern "social contract." For Hobbes, of course, the contract is entirely between individuals, and the sovereign is not a party to it. Hence, a "social contract" and "absolute sovereignty." The theory of "double contract"—the one between individuals which results in the creation of a "community" and the other between the community and its government (which Locke calls a "trust," rather than a contract)—can be attributed to Althusius and Pufendorf, among other Continental thinkers. However, the direct source of Locke's particular version of the twofold contract (or, strictly speaking, one contract and one trust) was probably Hooker.

It is easy to be confused about Locke's distinction of society (or community) and government—one for which he is indebted to Hooker probably more than anyone else—and this is largely due to Locke's own careless way of using terms. For instance, in this same chapter he says: "When any number of men have so consented to make one community or government," etc. But Locke cannot mean to say here that it is either "community" or "government," because they are not the same thing, nor are they created in the same way. He himself makes it clear in this chapter that community is created first, through a social contract, and that government is subsequently established by that community. "The beginning of politic society depends upon the consent of the individuals to join into, and make one society; who when they are thus incorporated," says he, "might set up what form of government they thought fit."

That society and government are two different things is made emphatically clear when Locke points out toward the end of this *Treatise* that a revolution which dissolves a government does not necessarily dissolve the society, or community, that such a situation does not necessarily revert men to the state of nature. In fact, the distinction of the two is the very key to Locke's theory of revolution, as will become clear later on.

The significant point about the contract-making, that is, the act through which men enter into society, is that once it is made it is final. That is to say, one cannot change his mind, upon, let us say, finding himself in the minority rather than majority, and ask to be excused from the decisions of the majority: "Whereas he that has once by actual agreement and any express declaration given his consent to be of any commonweal is perpetually and indispensably obliged to be and remain unalterably a subject to it, and can never be again in the liberty of the state of nature."

Locke also takes up some possible objections to his theory of the beginning of government. The first objection is that there is no record in history of government being formed by the consent of free men. Locke says there is no reason to assume, simply because we have no record of it, that government did not originate that way. Government, he points out, antedated records, and therefore there is no recording of the origin of it.

The second objection may be stated in this way: Since all men are born under government, it is impossible that any of them should be free to unite to form a new government. Locke answers that instances abound of new commonwealths being set up after men had broken off from older and larger ones. Some of the new commonwealths were, in fact, monarchies.

Locke then considers the question: what is a sufficient declaration of consent for entering society? He identifies two kinds of consent: express and tacit. With express consent there is no problem. If one openly declares himself to be a member of a given commonwealth, there can be no doubts about his intentions. With tacit consent, it is another matter. Just what is tacit consent, asks Locke, and how far does it bind? He has a ready answer: "And to this I say, that every man that hath any possession or enjoyment of any part of the dominions of government doth hereby give his tacit consent, and is as far forth obliged to obedience to the laws of that government, during such enjoyment, as any one under it, whether his possession be land to him and his heirs for ever, or a lodging only for a week; or whether it be barely travelling freely on the highway; and, in effect, it reaches as far as the very being of any one within the territories of that government." When one lives in a commonwealth by tacit agreement he may sell his property at any time and go live somewhere else. When he once lives in a commonwealth by express agreement he is obliged to remain forever a subject to his government.

Toward the end of this chapter Locke touches on a sticky problem: What is the proper scope of governmental jurisdiction over property? Locke's immediate answer will come as a surprise to anyone who looks upon him as the ideologist of the propertied class. Locke states very clearly that government should have jurisdiction over all private property. "For it would be a direct contradiction," he says, "for any one to enter into society with others for the securing and regulating of property, and yet to suppose his land, whose property is to be regulated by the laws of the society, should be exempt from the jurisdiction of that government to which he himself, and the property of the land, is a subject. By the same act, therefore, whereby any one unites his person, which was before free, to any commonwealth, by the same he unites his possessions, which were before free, to it also; and they become, both of them, person and possession, subject to the government and dominion of that commonwealth as long as it hath a being."

CHAPTER IX.   OF THE ENDS OF POLITICAL SOCIETY AND GOVERNMENT

> **COMMENT:**   Locke made such an astonishing statement in the last chapter—namely, that government has jurisdiction over all property in a commonwealth—that he finds it necessary in this chapter to qualify it. Government jurisdiction over property, of course, does not mean government ownership of it. But neither does it give any holder of private property the right to exclude government from regulating his holdings. The force of Locke's argument in the last chapter strikes squarely on the side of governmental authority in all matters relating to private property. If he had left it at that, his bourgeois friends would surely have been unhappy. But he does not. Rather, he puts as the chief end of uniting into commonwealth the preservation of property. And property is, again, curiously enough, defined as "life, liberty, and estate."

In Chapter VI Locke equated paternal power with paternal responsibility. In other words, the power of parents over their children derives from their responsibility to see to their children's good. Now Locke extends this argument to political power of government over its people. The government in a political society has power over all property of its subjects. But the preservation of that property is the chief aim of government. So the power of government over property is contingent upon the government's carrying out its responsibility to preserve it. But if one is free in the state of nature, asks Locke, why does he part with his natural freedom and enter into a commonwealth? The answer is that that freedom is at best a precarious one. Locke gives three reasons: first, there is no established, known law in the state of nature, received by common consent, as a standard of right and wrong, to settle disputes. Although the law of nature is known to "reasonable creatures," such as men are, self-interest and ignorance lead them to disregard it. Second, there is no known impartial judge with authority to settle differences according to the established law. Third, there is no power to support and execute sentences once they are pronounced.

Thus, everyone, having in the state of nature the powers of self-preservation and of punishment of those who transgress against the law of nature, now gives up these powers upon entering the commonwealth. But the power of the political society is never to extend beyond its original aim: protection of the properties of its members against the defects of the state of nature.

CHAPTER X.   OF THE FORMS OF A COMMONWEALTH

This is a short chapter, and will be treated in kind. Locke identifies three forms of government: democracy, oligarchy, and monarchy. He defines democracy as a form of government in which the majority employs the power of the community to make laws and to execute them by officers of their own appointing. Oligarchy is such power possessed by a few, and monarchy, by one. Two kinds of monarchy are listed: hereditary and elective.

It is also conceivable, says Locke, that the community make "compounded and mixed forms of government, as they think good." In any case, the form of government depends on where the supreme, or legislative, power is placed.

CHAPTER XI.   OF THE EXTENT OF THE LEGISLATIVE POWER

"The first and fundamental positive law of all commonwealths," says Locke, "is the establishment of the legislative power." This legislative power is governed by "the first and fundamental natural law," which is (1) the preservation of the society and (2) the preservation of every person in it. Locke designates to this body the title *supreme power,* i.e., supreme power of the commonwealth. It is, he says, both "sacred and unalterable in the hands where the community has once placed it." The scope of this power is such that no edict of anyone else or of any other group can have the force and obligation of a law, if that edict does not have its sanction from the legislative which the community has chosen.

Yet, the legislative cannot arbitrarily determine the lives and fortunes of the people, because it is "but the joint power of every member of the society given up to that person, or assembly. . . ." And that power being "no more than those persons had in a state of nature before they entered into society, and gave it up to the community," no one can be expected to "transfer to another more power than he has in himself; and nobody has an absolute arbitrary power over himself, or over any other to destroy his own life, or take away the life or property of another."

Consequently, the power of the legislative is *limited* to that which is necessary to produce the public good and the preservation of the community. It cannot be used to destroy, enslave, or impoverish the subjects. The rules which the legislators make for other men's actions, as well as their own, must conform to the law of nature. And since the fundamental law of nature is the preservation of mankind, the law of the legislative cannot contradict that end.

Locke gives two arguments against arbitrary government. The first is the argument from the law of nature, which has just been stated. The second is the argument from individual intent, or motive. The latter argument is as follows. He says that if the legislative were to be given arbitrary power over the people, that people would be in "a worse condition than the state of nature, wherein they had a liberty to defend their right against the injuries of others, and were upon equal terms to maintain it, whether invaded by a single man or many in combination." Not only would the legislative have more power with which to prey on the people than any individual in the state of nature; but whereas in the state of nature an individual, at least, has the liberty to protect himself by force of arms, in civil society he cannot do so because he has disarmed himself. Consequently, says Locke, "it cannot be supposed that they should intend, had they a power to do so, to give to any one, or more, an absolute arbitrary power over their persons and estates, and put a force into the magistrate's hand to execute his unlimited will arbitrarily upon them."

Locke also says that the supreme power cannot take from any-one part of his property without his own consent. "The preservation of property being the end of government, and that for which men enter into society," says Locke, "it necessarily supposes and requires that the people should have property, without which they must be supposed to lose that by entering into society, which was the end for which they entered into it, too gross an absurdity for any man to own."

COMMENT: This does not, however, contradict Locke's earlier statement in defense of property regulation. There has only been a shift of emphasis. That a political society is constituted to protect property and that the supreme power cannot take away one's possession without his consent is a foregone conclusion. Locke was just pointing out, in Chapter VIII, that *protection* involves *regulation* (but regulation does not involve government ownership).

On balance, Locke's uncompromising defense of the sanctity and inviolability of private property stands beyond dispute. In this same chapter he declares that although military commanders have power of life and death over their soldiers, they have no power of taking money from them. "We see," says he, "that neither the sergeant, that could command a soldier to march up to the mouth of a cannon, or stand in a breach, where he is almost sure to perish, can command that soldier to give him one penny of his money; nor the general, that can condemn him to death for deserting his post, or not obeying the most desperate orders, cannot [sic] yet, with all his absolute power of life and death, dispose of one farthing of that soldier's estate, or seize one jot of his goods, whom yet he can command anything, and hang for the least disobedience."

Locke then goes on to say that the legislative authority must dispense justice and decide the rights of its subjects through known laws and authorized judges—a commonplace of political theory, which can be found in St. Thomas Aquinas, Hobbes, and many others. Locke also emphasizes the fact that the legislative is a "delegated power from the people." This means that those who are entrusted with that power "cannot pass it over to others." Only the people—or, strictly speaking, the majority of the community—have the power to decide where the legislative power should reside.

CHAPTER XII. OF THE LEGISLATIVE, EXECUTIVE, AND FEDERATIVE POWER OF THE COMMONWEALTH

This brief chapter distinguishes the *legislative, executive,* and *federative* powers of government. The fundamental principle of the separation of powers is expressed in the following words: "Because it may be too great a temptation to human frailty, apt to grasp at power for the same persons, who have the power of making laws, to have also in their hands the power to execute them, whereby they exempt themselves from obedience to the laws they make, and suit the law, both in its making and execution to their own private advantage, and thereby come to have a distinct interest from the rest of the community, contrary to the end of society and government."

However, one must bear in mind that Locke is applying this noble principle only to the separation of the *legislative* and *executive* functions. He says nothing about the judicial branch. Therefore, to attribute to Locke a theory of separation of powers, with checks and balances, in the sense that we understand it today is a mistake.

> **COMMENT:** The author of the theory of separation of powers, in its modern version, is not Locke but Montesquieu. It is the theory of Montesquieu, not that of Locke, that James Madison was lecturing on in the forty-seventh paper of *The Federalist,* in defense of the Constitutional provisions for the separation of powers.

Locke does, however, distinguish one other political power—and one suspects that this is the main source of the misunderstanding just alluded to—namely, "the power of war and peace, leagues and alliances." Locke calls this the *federative power.* But though the executive and federative powers are "distinct in themselves," they must nevertheless be placed in the same hands. This is because foreign policy is generally not susceptible to being guided by antecedent positive laws, but must instead be guided *ad hoc* from event to event by prudence and wisdom.

CHAPTER XIII. OF THE SUBORDINATION OF THE POWERS OF THE COMMONWEALTH

> **COMMENT:** In Chapter XI Locke said that the *supreme power* of the commonwealth rests in the hands of the legislative. In this chapter, however, he tells us that the supreme power remains in the people. This may sound a bit confusing, but if so, it is necessary. For in this apparent contradiction lies the crux of Locke's liberal political theory, which is based on a distinction between *society under government* and *society without government.*

"Though in a constituted commonwealth . . . there can be but one supreme power, which is the legislative," says Locke, "there remains still in the people a supreme power to remove or alter the legislative when they find the legislative act contrary to the trust reposed in them." This, he tells us, follows from the obvious fact that the legislative power being a trust for the attainment of a certain end, "whenever that is manifestly neglected or opposed, the trust must necessarily be forfeited." In this sense, "the community perpetually retains a supreme power of saving themselves from the attempts and designs of any body, even of their legislators whenever they shall be so foolish or wicked as to lay and carry on designs against the liberties and properties of the subject."

> **COMMENT:**   Locke does not mean, however, that the community may exercise the supreme power in opposition to the legislative. That would be a flat contradiction, for we cannot have two supreme powers at the same time. Instead, what he means is this. When the community exercises its supreme power, it is presumed that the legitimate government has ceased to exist: "The community may be said in this respect to be always the supreme power, but not as considered under any form of government, because this power of the people can never take place till government be dissolved." In other words, the community exercises the supreme power only in *society without government;* but as long as government is in operation, the supreme power is in the hands of the legislative, where the people have placed it.
>
> If the government should be dissolved, the people—i.e., the majority of the community—will once again resume and exercise their supreme power—to form a new government by placing the legislative power in new hands.

Locke then outlines the principle of legislative supremacy over the executive. He makes it quite clear that the legislative creates the executive, and goes on to say that "when the legislative hath put the execution of the laws they make into other hands, they have a power still to resume it out of those hands, when they find cause, and to punish for any mal-administration against the laws. The same holds also in regard of the federative power, that and the executive being both ministerial and subordinate to the legislative which, as has been shown, in a constituted commonwealth is supreme."

Locke then discusses some of the powers and functions of the executive. He has the power of convoking the legislative, when it is not convoked by statute, but must do so always for the public good. He must not use this power to the detriment of the community. The executive is in possession of the force of the commonwealth, and could theoretically use it to hinder or prevent the meeting of the legislative, that is, he could use it tyrannically. But Locke is once again quite clear on this point. "In all states and conditions," he says, "the true remedy of force without authority is to oppose force to it. The use of force without authority always puts him that uses it into a state of war, as the aggressor, and renders him liable to be treated accordingly." And he says specifically that "though the executive power may have the prerogative of convoking and dissolving such conventions of the legislative, yet it is not thereby superior to it."

Another of the powers of the executive is quite interesting and has a distinctly contemporary flavor. Locke says that "it often comes to pass that in governments where part of the legislative consists of representatives chosen by the people, that in tract of time this representation becomes very unequal and disproportionate to the reason it was at first established upon."

The people cannot remedy this situation because, once the legislative is constituted, they have no power to act so long as the government stands. The remedy therefore must be found in executive action, and his action, based on his "prerogative power," is essentially that of redistricting the country. When convoking the assembly he "regulates not by old custom but true reason the number of members in all the places that have a right to be distinctly represented." In doing so he "cannot be judged to have set up a new legislative, but to have restored the old and true one."

CHAPTER XIV.   OF PREROGATIVE

The executive may act not only without the sanction of the law; he may also make the laws "give way" to his power where blind adherence to them would be harmful, and he may even go so far as to act contrary to the laws for the public good. "This power to act according to discretion for the public good, without the prescription of the law and sometimes even against it, is that which is called *prerogative*."

> **COMMENT:**   It must be remembered in considering Locke's discussion of this point that the power of prerogative was possessed by the English monarch of his time; it was his personal power in running the state. The Civil War had occurred largely as an outgrowth of the republicans' objections to the excesses of the royal prerogative, as it was exercised against the Parliament.

Locke observes historically that in its infancy government was almost all prerogative, and he says that a good prince cannot have too much prerogative. But he also points out that "it is impossible that anybody in the society should ever have a right to do people harm," and that "prerogative is nothing but the power of doing public good without a rule." In this connection he puts forward an interesting and strictly utilitarian view of the nature and purpose of punishment. "The end of government being the preservation of all as much as may be," says he, "even the guilty are to be spared where it can prove no prejudice to the innocent." Locke also says that the power of calling parliament in England is an example of prerogative, and the implication is that the power of redistricting, which has been discussed above, would also be in this category.

The obvious problem arising with respect to prerogative is: who shall judge when this power is used properly? Locke claims that when the executive or the legislative oversteps its bounds, "there can be no judge on earth" to decide this question. And then in a curious passage he hints at the right of revolution by using such expressions as "reserved" powers of the people and of their right to "appeal to heaven." When the government has betrayed the original purpose of its institution, Locke says, "the people have no other remedy in this, as in all other cases where they have no judge on earth, but to appeal to heaven." He goes on to say that the people "have reserved that ultimate determination to themselves which belongs to all mankind, where there lies no appeal on earth, by a law antecedent and paramount to all positive laws of men, whether they have just cause to make their appeal to heaven."

Locke has thus raised the specter of revolution, which Hobbes had tried so vigorously to exorcise. But he is quick to calm the fears of the worried reader, for he adds: "Nor let anyone think this lays a perpetual foundation for disorder, for this operates not till the inconvenience is so great that the majority feel it and are weary of it, and find a necessity to have it amended."

CHAPTER XV.   OF PATERNAL, POLITICAL, AND DESPOTICAL POWER CONSIDERED TOGETHER

This chapter deals with a comparative definition of three types of power: paternal, political, and despotical. *Paternal,* or parental, *power* refers simply to the governance of the parent over their children till they have reached the age where they have sufficient reason and knowledge to "understand that rule, whether it be the law of nature or the municipal law of their country, they are to govern themselves by." Locke maintains that this is a *natural government,* rather than a political government, and that the power of the parent does not reach to the property of the child, who alone has the right to dispose of it.

Political power is that which men surrender into the hands of the community, or society, as they leave the state of nature and which is thereupon entrusted to the government—"with this express or tacit trust that it shall be employed for their good and the preservation of their property." This is a twofold power. It involves, in the first place, the power to use "such means for the preservation of his own property as he thinks good and nature allows him." Secondly, it is the power "to punish the breach of the law of nature in others so as, according to the best of his reason, may most conduce to the preservation of himself and the rest of mankind."

> **COMMENT:**   Locke then goes on to make the point, which he constantly emphasizes, that since the only end of government is the preservation of the property of those who have created it, "it can have no other end or measure when in the hands of the magistrates but to preserve the members of that society in their lives, liberties, and possessions; and so cannot be an absolute, arbitrary power over their lives and fortunes, which are as much as possible to be observed, but a power to make laws, and annex such penalties to them as may tend to the preservation of the whole. . . ."

The third kind of power is *despotical power*. This is "an absolute power one man has over another to take away his life whenever he pleases." According to Locke, this is a power which is neither the gift of nature nor the product of a compact, "for man, not having such an arbitrary power over his own life, cannot give another man such a power over it." Instead, says Locke, it is "the effect only of forfeiture which the aggressor makes of his own life when he puts himself into the state of war with another." It is the aggressor in war, who, "having quitted reason, which God hath given to be the rule between man and man," puts himself in danger of being the victim of despotical power. "And thus," continues Locke, "captives, taken in a just and lawful war, and such only, are subject to a despotical power, which, as it arises not from compact, so neither is it capable of any, but is the state of war continued."

Nature is the source of paternal power, *voluntary agreement* the source of political power, and *forfeiture* the source of despotical power. And Locke concludes this chapter with these words: "Absolute dominion, however placed, is so far from being one kind of civil society that it is as inconsistent with it as slavery is with property." The obvious contrast is, of course, with Hobbes' theory of absolute sovereignty, against which Locke is consciously writing.

CHAPTER XVI. OF CONQUEST

In this chapter, Locke deals with the meaning of conquest, of just and unjust war, and of the relationship between right and might. He starts with a reiteration of the doctrine of *consent* as the necessary basis of lawful government. He finds it lamentable that so many people have confounded the force of arms with the consent of the people and have, consequently, attributed the origins of government to conquest. The sole basis of government, he insists, is the consent of the people.

Locke then makes an interesting comment about the famous "appeal to heaven." "And he that appeals to heaven," says Locke, "must be sure he has right on his side; and a right, too, that is worth the trouble and cost of his appeal, as he will answer at a tribunal that cannot be deceived, and will be sure to retribute to everyone according to the mischiefs he hath created to his fellow-subjects, that is, any part of mankind." It is clear that Locke was not advocating indiscriminate rebellion. In fact, he was being rather cautious. In this respect, i.e., in his cautious attitude toward rebellion, Locke was not much different from St. Thomas Aquinas.

What does Locke mean when he speaks of one's duty to be sure that "he has right on his side"? What difference does it make? It makes a difference, Locke says, because not all wars are alike. There are just and unjust wars, and there are just and unjust parties to the same war.

This takes us to Locke's discussion of conquest proper. In the same way that there is a distinction between just and unjust war, so there is a difference between a lawful and an unlawful conqueror. "The power a conqueror gets over those he overcomes in a just war," says Locke, "is perfectly despotical; he has an absolute power over the lives of those, who by putting themselves in a state of war, have forfeited them." But, Locke adds, "he has not thereby a right and title to their possessions."

Locke concedes that his argument will seem "a strange doctrine, it being so quite contrary to the practice of the world." But, he argues, "the practice of the strong and powerful, how universal soever it may be, is seldom the rule of right." Later in this same chapter, Locke sums up his views in the following words: "The government of a conqueror, imposed by force on the subdued, against whom he had no right of war, or who joined not in the war against him, where he had right, has no obligation upon them."

> **COMMENT:**   The argument of this chapter is directed against Hobbes. Hobbes said that commonwealths originate in two ways: (1) by institution and (2) by acquisition. What distinguishes a commonwealth by institution from a commonwealth by acquisition is that the former is brought about through a covenant of every man with every other man, while the latter is made by force. Does force make a commonwealth illegitimate? Hobbes' answer is no; he says force is not inconsistent with consent. In Chapter XIV of *Leviathan,* he makes it clear that "covenants entered into by fear, in the condition of mere nature, are obligatory." In other words, even if one enters into a contract out of fear, he is bound fully to carry out the terms of the contract. Despite his fear, he consented to it. Hence, it was a voluntary action. This is the way it is, for Hobbes, in a commonwealth by acquisition: "I am bound by it, for it is a contract, wherein one receives the benefit of life."

Later, in Chapter XX of *Leviathan* Hobbes makes a similar statement. In a commonwealth by acquisition as in a commonwealth by institution, "men singly, or many together by plurality of voices, for fear of death, or bonds, *authorize* all the actions of that man, or assembly, that hath their lives and liberty in his power" (emphasis added).

The only difference between a commonwealth by institution and a commonwealth by acquisition is that in one instance people choose their sovereign for fear of one another whereas in the other case "they subject themselves to him they are afraid of." The point is that in both cases the motivation behind adopting political obligation is fear, and, consequently, such a decision is a *voluntary act*. Therefore, "the rights and consequences of sovereignty, are the same in both."

It is wrong to assume, as some have done, that Hobbes saw no distinction between might and right: that for Hobbes might gives rise to right, whereas for Locke might and right are distinct and separate. On the contrary, both believed that the only moral basis of government is *consent*. They differ merely on the definition of consent, and the meaning of free choice. Hobbes says in Chapter XXI of *Leviathan* that "fear and liberty" and "liberty and necessity" are consistent. Locke thought this to be impossible.

CHAPTER XVII.   OF USURPATION

Usurpation is "a change only of persons, but not of the forms and rules of government." A usurper is defined as "whoever gets into the exercise of any part of the [government] power, by other ways than what the laws of the community have prescribed. . . . " The usurper has no claim to obedience until the people consent to his rule.

CHAPTER XVIII.   OF TYRANNY

Tyranny is defined simply as the exercise of power without right, and more elaborately as the use of power, not for the common good, but for the private ends of whoever is in power.

Locke quotes King James I to the effect that "a king governing in a settled kingdom, leaves to be a king and degenerates into a tyrant, as soon as he leaves off to rule according to his laws." And Locke himself adds: "Wherever law ends tyranny begins, if the law be transgressed to another's harm." The last qualifying phrase here is inserted with the notion of prerogative power in mind. In Chapter XIV, Locke says that the executive may exercise prerogative power even against the law, so long as it is used for the general good.

Locke says that the "appeal to heaven" will be rare, and adds that "the person of the prince by the law is sacred." He says further that "the right of resisting, even in manifest acts of tyranny, will not suddenly or on slight occasions disturb the government; for if it reach no further than some private men's cases . . . yet the right to [defend themselves] will not easily engage them in a contest wherein they are sure to perish. . . ." Moreover, "if either these illegal acts have extended to the majority of the people, or if the mischief and oppression has lighted only on some few . . . and they are persuaded in their consciences that their laws, and with them their estates, liberties, and lives are in danger . . . how they will be hindered from resisting illegal force used against them, I cannot tell."

CHAPTER XIX. OF THE DISSOLUTION OF GOVERNMENT

COMMENT: All major traditional political thinkers, from Plato to Hobbes, were concerned about the dissolution of government. So it is with Locke. But Locke's concern is different from that of the others. They sought to examine the forces contributing to the decay of government; Locke seeks only to examine whether the dissolution of government is right and moral, and if so, under what circumstances. They were interested in the phenomenon of dissolution; he is interested in its justification. They asked, what causes government to change? He asks whether it is right to change government. And, if so, when should this right be exercised?

Locke first distinguishes between the dissolution of the society and the dissolution of the government. Needless to say, Hobbes would not have recognized such a distinction as meaningful. For him, the dissolution of the government meant at once the dissolution of the society, for he could not imagine how people could possibly live together as a group except under the watchful eye of the sovereign. For Locke, however, the distinction is quite meaningful, and even logically necessary, because a society and a government are created through entirely different procedures: one through a *social contract* and the other through a *trust.* The society may exist even after the government has been dissolved, for the existence of the former is not contingent upon that of the latter, while the latter cannot exist without the former.

"The usual and almost only way" the society, or community, is dissolved, says Locke, is "the inroad of foreign force making a conquest upon them." When this happens, we are told, everyone returns to the original state of nature, "with a liberty to shift for himself and provide for his own safety, as he thinks fit, in some other society."

The dissolution of society implies and includes the dissolution of government, for the latter is built on the foundation of the former: "There wants not much argument to prove that where the society is dissolved, the government cannot remain—that being as impossible as for the frame of a house to subsist when the materials of it are scattered and dissipated by a whirlwind, or jumbled into a confused heap by an earthquake."

However, a government can be dissolved from within, that is to say, without the dissolution of the society over which it exists. There are several kinds of dissolution of government. The first occurs "when the legislative is altered." Locke notes that the establishment of the legislative body is the first and fundamental act of a society, and, consequently, "when any one or more shall take upon them to make laws, whom the people have not appointed so to do, they make laws without authority, which the people are not therefore bound to obey." Likewise, Locke continues, "Every one is at the disposure of his own will when those who had by the delegation of the society the declaring of the public will are excluded from it, and others usurp the place who have no such authority or delegation." When the government is so dissolved, says Locke, the people, i.e., the majority of the community, are at liberty to give themselves a new legislature.

Locke then lists several situations where the legislative has been altered, that is to say, the government dissolved: (1) when a single person or prince sets up his own arbitrary will in place of the laws which are the will of the society declared by the legislative; (2) when the prince hinders the legislative from assembling in its due time, or from acting freely pursuant to those ends for which it was constituted; (3) when, by the arbitrary power of the prince, the electors or ways of election are altered without the consent, and contrary to the common interest of the people; and (4) when the people are delivered into the subjection of a foreign power. Locke then adds one more situation where he who has the supreme executive power neglects and abandons that charge, whereby the laws already made are no longer put into execution.

The second major category of cases in which the government is dissolved from within has to do with the situation where "the legislative or the prince, either of them, act contrary to their trust." The legislative acts against the trust when it endeavors to invade the property of the subject, and to make itself master or arbitrary disposer of the lives, liberties, or fortunes of the people. When the legislative acts in such a way—which Locke describes as a "breach of trust"—it puts itself "into a state of war with the people who are thereupon absolved from any further obedience." Now the people may resume their "original liberty" as a community and establish a new legislative body— "such as they shall think fit, provided for their own safety and security, which is the end for which they are in society."

As for the executive, violation of the trust takes a dual form, for that branch of government bears, as Locke calls it, a *double trust*, "both to have a part in the legislative and the supreme execution of the law." For this reason, he will be acting against both these trusts "when he goes about to set up his own arbitrary will as the law of the society."

Locke then undertakes to resolve two important questions relating to rebellion: What are the chances of a rebellion occurring? And, what is its moral justification? To the possible charge that his theory "lays a ferment for frequent rebellion" Locke first calls our attention to the "slowness and aversion in the people to quit their old constitutions" and goes on to say: "I answer, such revolutions happen not upon every little mismanagement in public affairs. Great mistakes in the ruling part, many wrong and inconvenient laws, and all the slips of human frailty will be borne by the people without any mutiny or murmur." But, he continues, "if a long train of abuses, prevarications, and artifices, all tending the same way, make the design visible to the people, and they cannot but feel what they lie under, and see whither they are going, 'tis not to be wondered that they should then rouse themselves, and endeavour to put the rule into such hands which may secure to them the ends for which government was at first erected, and without which, ancient names and specious forms are so far from being better, that they are much worse than the state of nature or pure anarchy; the inconveniences being all as great and as near, but the remedy farther off and more difficult."

> **COMMENT:** Needless to say, Locke had Hobbes in mind when he wrote this passage. And Hobbes would take strong objection especially to Locke's last point, because it would be unthinkable to Hobbes that a civil society with a government over it, no matter how tyrannical it may be, could become "much worse than the state of nature or pure anarchy." For Hobbes, any government would be better than no government at all.

Locke continues his analysis of rebellion by claiming that his doctrine, far from laying a ferment for frequent rebellion, "is the best fence against" and "the probablest means to hinder it."

> COMMENT: This seemingly strange contention is justi-
> fied—with perhaps a rather precarious logic—by the
> statement that the rebellion is commited not by the peo-
> ple who resist and overthrow a tyrannical government,
> but rather by that government in becoming tyrannical in
> the first place. Locke says: "For rebellion being an oppo-
> sition, not to persons, but authority, which is founded only
> in the constitutions and laws of the government; those
> whoever they be, who by force break through, and by force
> justify their violation of them, are truly and properly reb-
> els." This is a noble doctrine, but it is difficult to see how
> the government, which is the sole possessor of the "su-
> preme power" (while, that is, the government is in ex-
> istence), can at the same time be a rebel. If Locke had
> stayed with his original terminology "breach of trust," he
> would have avoided this unnecessary confusion. Then, a
> breach would be an act committed by the government
> against the community, while a rebellion would be one
> undertaken by the community against the unfaithful gov-
> ernment.

Locke also gives the following answer, with tongue in cheek, to the absolutist doctrine of Hobbes, and, as usual, without mentioning his name: "Who would not think it an admirable peace betwixt the mighty and the mean when the lamb without resistance yielded his throat to be torn by the imperious wolf. Polyphemus' den gives us a perfect pattern of such a peace and such a government, wherein Ulysses and his companions had nothing to do but quietly to suffer themselves to be devoured. And no doubt Ulysses, who was a prudent man, preached up passive obedience, and exhorted them to a quiet submission by representing to them of what concernment peace was to man-kind, and by showing the inconveniences which might happen if they should offer to resist Polyphemus, who had now the power over them."

But the cautious Locke is quick to add, once again, that resistance will not come "till the mischief be grown general," and till the people "universally have a persuasion grounded upon manifest evidence" that the government is unbearably tyrannical. But the fact remains that in the case of the exercise of "force without right," Locke tells us, "all former ties are cancelled."

Now, Locke asks, "If a controversy arise betwixt a prince and some of the people in a matter where the law is silent or doubtful, and the thing to be of great consequence, I should think the proper umpire in such a case should be the body of the people. . . . But if the prince . . . decline that way of determination, the appeal lies nowhere but to heaven." In other words, in case of a controversy between the government and some private citizens where the law is not explicit, the power of determining who is right should reside in the people as a whole (i.e., the community by majority rule). But if the government refuses to abide by this procedure (i.e., allowing the people to be judge), then "the appeal lies nowhere but to heaven."

> **COMMENT:**   Obviously, the meaning of the term "appeal to heaven" is crucial. Does it mean that the people must kneel down and pray to God? No. If that were the meaning, then the people would relinquish political power, and Locke never suggests that the people (i.e., the community) should ever do so.
>
> Does it mean that the people must ask permission from the government to rebel against it? No. That cannot be the case for the same reason. Besides, it would be absurd for Locke to suggest that the people have a right to rebel, and then, in effect, to take away the right by putting as a condition of rebellion that they first ask permission of the government.

But there is one other possible interpretation of the term "appeal to heaven." The government was set up in the first place as a fiduciary power. This means it can only carry out the duties entrusted to it by the community. In the event of controversy between the government and some citizens, if the government refuses to recognize that the people as a whole should be judge then it is refusing at the same time to accept its role as trustee. In other words, it is refusing to recognize the ultimate supremacy of the community. So if it attempts to enforce its will on the community it uses force without right and puts itself in a state of war with the community. This gives legitimacy to the people's right to rebel.

It also means that there remains no power on earth to decide the controversy. So each side must "appeal to heaven" to determine for itself what is right, in other words, *make its own determination of the law of nature*. The laws of nature, which are also precepts of reason, are the will of God. Therefore, appealing to heaven in this case means using the faculty of reason to determine what is the will of God. This seems to be what Locke was trying to say when he used the term "appeal to heaven," rather than to pray or ask permission of the government to rebel.

But this leads us to a problem of a different nature. With the absence of a common judge on earth, and with each side appealing to heaven, then we have reverted to a condition which for all practical purposes is no different from the state of nature. So Locke is inadvertently admitting that the state of war and the state of nature are really the same thing. If this interpretation is correct, it means that even in the absence of foreign conquest, not only the government, but the whole community, or politic society, may be dissolved. This is a point which Locke had been at great pains to deny in his efforts to refute Hobbes' theory of absolute sovereignty.

In conclusion, it may be noted that Locke was the first major thinker in the history of political theory to formulate an explicit theory of a right of revolution. Locke's theory of revolution is a logical consequence of his belief in natural law in its traditional conception, that is, Stoic and medieval. For him the moral order has an objective and timeless quality, and man's political order must be patterned, ideally, after this higher order and its standards. No doubt, something of this argument can be found in Plato's idealism, too. But the direct source of Locke's inspiration was the stoic-medieval conception of natural law.

It is not surprising to see, therefore, an implicit theory of revolution even in Cicero's thought, specifically his conception of two commonwealths. One commonwealth is of the state, the other of the universe. Each person, being a member of both these commonwealths, obeys both the civil law of the state and the natural law of the universe. If, says Cicero, the civil law should come in conflict with the natural law, then the citizens must always obey the latter. But he does not say just how they should go about disobeying the civil law. Even so, it is clear that Cicero had said enough to lay the foundation for the theory that Locke stated in this chapter. In light of our previous comments, it is questionable whether Locke succeeded in finally settling the problem.

ESSAY QUESTIONS AND ANSWERS

1. According to Locke, how does property come into existence, and what is the role of government in its relation to property?

ANSWER: Locke's theory of property proceeds from two underlying assumptions: first, that the earth is common to all men, and, second, that each man has a property in his own person. *Labor* means the application of one's body (hence, his own person) to something that is originally neither his nor anyone else's—i.e., nature. Through labor, the private (person) and the public (nature) are joined together. For Locke, the fruit of the union is something that remains private, namely, property: the laborer "hath mixed his labor with and joined to it something that is his own, and thereby makes it his property." Moreover, one can accumulate all the property he can use without it going to waste.

When Locke moves on to his discussion of the relation of property to government, he redefines the term "property" to include all things indispensable to decent human existence, hence, "life, liberty, and estate." In the state of nature, Locke tells us, property is "very unsafe, very insecure." It is to remedy this state of affairs that men enter into civil society. Thus, "the greatest and chief end . . . of men's uniting into commonwealths and putting themselves under government is the preservation of their property."

It follows logically that when a government fails to live up to its trust, by endeavoring to "invade the property of the subject, and to make itself master or arbitrary disposer of the lives, liberties, or fortunes of the people," it puts itself into a state of war with the people by using force without right. In such an event, says Locke, the people are "absolved from any further obedience."

2. What is the significance of the idea of civil society, or "community," in Locke's theory of social contract?

ANSWER: For Locke, "social contract" is the method of creating a civil society, or "community," which, in turn, establishes a government. Through social contract men in the state of nature agree with one another to surrender their original legislative and executive powers—i.e., the legislative power of the individual "to do whatsoever he thinks fit for the preservation of himself and others within the permission of the law of nature," and his executive power "to punish the crimes committed against the law"—into the hands of the community. By virtue of this contract, the community gains the *supreme power* (which is comparable to Hobbes' "sovereignty").

The community is created for the express purpose of establishing a government, which is done through a *trust*. This means the government enjoys only a "fiduciary power." Nevertheless, once the government is created, the supreme power resides in it, and not in the community. This power reverts to the community, or people, only when the "government be dissolved." In the meantime, the "supreme power" possessed by the government remains latent in the people.

The will of the community is determined by the decision of its majority. In fact, when Locke speaks of "the people" he means the majority of the community.

Whereas, through the social contract, individuals surrender their natural legislative and executive powers to the community, the community (majority of the people) does not surrender these powers to the government. It merely entrusts them to the government without ever relinquishing them. Hence, the power of the community over its members is unlimited and, in a sense, absolute, whereas the power of government is limited and conditional. Men, once contracted into the community, can never leave it, except when it is dissolved through conquest by a foreign enemy. By contrast, the existence of government is entirely dependent upon that of the community.

The idea of community is the key to Locke's theory of revolution, because through the community the people can hold their government accountable to themselves. When the government acts in such a way as to commit a "breach of trust," it is said to war on the community, for the use of force without right is considered to be an act to war. By that very act, the government forfeits its legitimacy, and the people may resume their "original liberty" as a community in order to establish another government. They do this by calling on their "latent power" to dissolve the government, i.e., to make a revolution.

It should also be noted that "community" is not a description of any concrete political entity, but a pure analytical construct, designed specifically to articulate a theory of limited government.

SELECTED BIBLIOGRAPHY

THE PRINCIPAL WORKS OF LOCKE

Four *Letters Concerning Toleration*
    First Letter (Latin, 1685; English, 1689). Paperback.
    Second Letter (1690).
    Third Letter (1692).
    Fourth Letter (fragment, 1706).

Two Treatises of Government (1690). Paperback.

An Essay Concerning Human Understanding (1690), 4th ed., 1700.

Some Thoughts Concerning Education (1693).

The Reasonableness of Christianity as Delivered in the Scriptures (1695).

SELECTED RECENT WORKS ON LOCKE

Czajkowski, C. J., *The Theory of Private Property in John Locke's Political Philosophy* (Notre Dame, 1941).

Gough, J. W., *John Locke's Political Philosophy* (Oxford, 1950).

Kendall, Willmoore, *John Locke and the Doctrine of Majority Rule* (Urbana, Ill., 1941).

Lamprecht, Sterling, *The Moral and Political Philosophy of John Locke* (New York, 1918).

Larkin, Paschal, *Property in the Eighteenth Century, with a Special Reference to England and Locke* (London, 1930).

Macpherson, C. B., *The Politics of Possessive Individualism* (Oxford, 1962).

Plamenatz, John, *Man and Society* (New York, 1963) Vol. I, chap. 6.

Strauss Leo, and Cropsey, Joseph (eds.), *History of Political Philosophy* (Chicago, 1963), pp. 433-468.

NOTES

NOTES

NOTES

NOTES

NOTES

NOTES

ACHEBE - Things Fall Apart
AESCHYLUS - The Plays
ALBEE - Who's Afraid of Virginia Woolf
AQUINAS, ST. THOMAS - The Philosophy
ARISTOPHANES - The Plays
ARISTOTLE - The Philosophy
AUGUSTINE, ST. - The Works
AUSTEN - Emma/Mansfield Park
AUSTEN - Pride and Prejudice
BECKETT - Waiting for Godot
Beowulf
BRADBURY- The Martian Chronicles
BRECHT - The Plays
BRONTE - Jane Eyre
BRONTE - Wuthering Heights
BUCK - The Good Earth
CAMUS - The Stranger
CATHER - My Antonia
CERVANTES - Don Quixote
CHAUCER - Canterbury Tales
CHEKHOV - The Plays
CHOPIN - The Awakening
COLERIDGE - Rime of the Ancient Mariner
CONRAD - Heart of Darkness/Secret Sharer
CONRAD - Lord Jim
COOPER - Last of the Mohicans
CRANE - Red Badge of Courage
DANTE - The Divine Comedy
DE BEAUVOIR- Second Sex
DEFOE - Robinson Crusoe
DESCARTES - The Philosophy
DICKENS - Bleak House
DICKENS - David Copperfield
DICKENS - Great Expectations
DICKENS - Hard Times
DICKENS - Oliver Twist
DICKENS - A Tale of Two Cities
DICKINSON - The Poetry
DINESEN - Out of Africa
DOCTOROW- Ragtime
DONNE - The Poetry & The Metaphysical Poets
DOSTOYEVSKY - Brothers Karamazov
DREISER - Sister Carrie
ELIOT - Middlemarch
ELIOT - Silas Marner
ELIOT - Murder in the Cathedral & Poems
ELIOT - Waste Land
ELLISON - Invisible Man
EMERSON - Writings
EURIPIDES, AESCHYLUS, ARISTOPHANES -
The Plays
EURIPIDES - The Plays

FAULKNER - Absalom, Absalom!
FAULKNER - As I Lay Dying
FAULKNER - Light in August
FAULKNER - Sound and the Fury
FIELDING - Joseph Andrews
FIELDING - Tom Jones
FITZGERALD - The Great Gatsby
FITZGERALD - Tender is the Night
FLAUBERT - Madame Bovary/Three Tales
FORSTER - Passage to India/Howard's End
FRANK - Diary of a Young Girl
FREUD - Interpretation of Dreams
FROST - The Poetry
GARCIA-MARQUEZ - One Hundred Years of Solitude
GOETHE - Faust
GOLDING - Lord of the Flies
Greek and Roman Classics
Greek and Roman Classics
GREENE - Major Works
HAMMETT - The Maltese Falcon/Thin Man
HARDY - Far from the Madding Crowd
HARDY - The Mayor of Casterbridge
HARDY - Return of the Native
HARDY - Tess of the D'Urbervilles
HAWTHORNE - House of the Seven Gables/ Marble Faun
HAWTHORNE - The Scarlett Letter
HELLER - Catch-22
HEMINGWAY - A Farewell to Arms
HEMINGWAY - For Whom the Bell Tolls
HEMINGWAY - Major Works
HEMINGWAY - The Old Man and the Sea
HEMINGWAY - The Snows of Kilimanjaro
HEMINGWAY - The Sun Also Rises
HESSE - Siddhartha
HOMER - The Iliad
HOMER - The Odyssey
HUGO - Les Miserables
HUXLEY - Major Works
IBSEN - The Plays
JAMES - Portrait of a Lady
JAMES - The Turn of the Screw
JAMES - Washington Square
JOYCE - Portrait of the Artist as a Young Man
KAFKA - Major Works
KEATS - The Poetry
KESEY - One Flew Over the Cuckoo's Nest
KNOWLES - A Separate Peace
LAWRENCE - Sons & Lovers
LEE - To Kill a Mockingbird
LEGUIN - Left Hand of Darkness
LEWIS - Babbitt
LOCKE & HOBBES - The Philosophies

(Continued)

MONARCH NOTES
Available at Fine Bookstores Everywhere

(Continued)

LONDON - Call of the Wild
MACHIAVELLI - The Prince
MARLOWE - Dr. Faustus
Marxist & Utopian Socialists
MELVILLE - Billy Budd
MELVILLE - Moby Dick
MILLER - The Crucible/A View from the Bridge
MILLER - Death of a Salesman
MILTON - Paradise Lost
MOLIERE - The Plays
MORE - Utopia
MORRISON - Beloved
Mythology
The New Testament
The New Testament
NIETZSCHE - The Philosophy
The Old Testament as Living Literature
O'NEILL - Desire Under the Elms
O'NEILL - Long Day's Journey into Night
O'NEILL - The Plays
ORWELL - Animal Farm
ORWELL - 1984
PATON - Cry the Beloved Country
PLATO - The Republic and Selected Dialogues
POE - Tales and Poems
POPE - Rape of the Lock & Poems
RAWLINGS - The Yearling
REMARQUE - All Quiet on the Western Front
Rousseau & the 18th Century Philosophers
SALINGER - Catcher in the Rye
SALINGER - Franny & Zooey
SARTRE - No Exit/The Flies

SHAKESPEARE - Antony and Cleopatra
SHAKESPEARE - As You Like It
SHAKESPEARE - Hamlet
SHAKESPEARE - Henry IV, Part 1
SHAKESPEARE - Henry IV, Part 2
SHAKESPEARE - Henry V
SHAKESPEARE - Julius Caesar
SHAKESPEARE - King Lear
SHAKESPEARE - Macbeth
SHAKESPEARE - The Merchant of Venice
SHAKESPEARE - A Midsummer Night's Dream
SHAKESPEARE - Othello
SHAKESPEARE - Richard II
SHAKESPEARE - Richard III
SHAKESPEARE - Romeo and Juliet

SHAKESPEARE - Selected Comedies
SHAKESPEARE - Sonnets
SHAKESPEARE - Taming of the Shrew
SHAKESPEARE - Tempest
SHAKESPEARE - Winter's Tale
SHAKESPEARE - Twelfth Night

SHAW - Major Plays
SHAW - Pygmalion
SHAW - Saint Joan
SINCLAIR - The Jungle
Sir Gawain and the Green Knight
SKINNER - Walden Two
SOLZHENITSYN - One Day in the Life of Ivan Denisovich
SOPHOCLES - The Plays
SPENSER - The Faerie Queene
STEINBECK - The Grapes of Wrath
STEINBECK - Major Works
STEINBECK - Of Mice and Men
STEINBECK - The Pearl/Red Pony
SWIFT - Gulliver's Travels
THACKERAY - Vanity Fair/Henry Esmond
THOREAU - Walden
TOLKEIN - Fellowship of the Ring
TOLSTOY - War and Peace
TURGENEV - Fathers and Sons
TWAIN - Huckleberry Finn
TWAIN - Tom Sawyer
UPDIKE - Rabbit Run/Rabbit Redux
VIRGIL - Aeneid
VOLTAIRE - Candide/The Philosophies
VONNEGUT - Slaughterhouse Five
WALKER - The Color Purple
WARREN - All the King's Men
WAUGH - Major Works
WELLS - Invisible Man/War of the Worlds
WHARTON - Ethan Frome
WHITMAN - Leaves of Grass
WILDE - The Plays
WILDER - Our Town/Bridge of San Luis Rey
WILLIAMS - The Glass Menagerie
WILLIAMS - Major Plays
WILLIAMS - A Streetcar Named Desire
WOLFE - Look Homeward, Angel/Of Time and the River
WOOLF - Mrs. Dalloway/To the Lighthouse
WORDSWORTH - The Poetry
WRIGHT - Native Son
YEATS - The Poetry
ZOLA - Germinal

PRENTICE HALL